GOD

AND THE CIVIL GOVERNMENT

MAGISTRATES, ELECTIONS, AND THE
DUTIES OF CITIZENS AND RULERS

FURTHER WORKS BY JOHN CALVIN AND PIERRE VIRET

A Light to My Path: An Exposition on the Ten Commandment

Defend the Truth: a Conversation on the Ninth Commandment

Honor thy Father and Mother

No Other God: A Practical Look at a Personal God

Nothing Like God: A Penetrating Application of the Second Commandment

Remember the Sabbath Day

Taking His Name in Vain

Thou Shalt Not Commit Adultery

Thou Shalt Not Covet

Thou Shalt Not Kill: A Plea for Life

Thou Shalt Not Steal

For a full listing of available titles, please visit:
psalm78ministries.com

GOD

AND THE CIVIL GOVERNMENT

MAGISTRATES, ELECTIONS, AND THE

DUTIES OF CITIZENS AND RULERS

by John Calvin

Translated by R. A. Sheats

Psalm 78 Ministries

www.psalm78ministries.com

God and the Civil Government: Magistrates, elections, and the duties of citizens and rulers

by John Calvin

Translated by R. A. Sheats

Published by:

Psalm 78 Ministries
P. O. Box 950
Monticello, FL 32345

psalm78ministries.com

Biblical quotations are taken from the King James Version of the Holy Scriptures.

TABLE OF CONTENTS

And Moses' father in law said unto him, The thing that thou doest is not good. Thou wilt surely wear away, both thou, and this people that is with thee: for this thing is too heavy for thee; thou art not able to perform it thyself alone. Hearken now unto my voice, I will give thee counsel, and God shall be with thee: Be thou for the people to God-ward, that thou mayest bring the causes unto God: and thou shalt teach them ordinances and laws, and shalt shew them the way wherein they must walk, and the work that they must do. Moreover thou shalt provide out of all the people able men, such as fear God, men of truth, hating covetousness; and place such over them, to be rulers of thousands, and rulers of hundreds, rulers of fifties, and rulers of tens: and let them judge the people at all seasons.

— Exodus 18:17-22

Translator's Note

From the duties of Christians at the ballot box to the doctrine of the lesser magistrate, John Calvin (1509-1564) had much to say on the institution and workings of civil government. Included in this volume are his thoughts on elections, rulers, judges, and civil office. His writings discuss the role of God's law in jurisprudence and stipulate the standards by which nations must be governed. He examines just magistrates and tyrants, honor and obedience, and the overruling hand of providence found in all offices and positions of authority. He also issues a biblical warning against fearing men or favoring an unjust cause in judgment.

Pertinent in its thought and stunning in its applicability to contemporary law and politics, Calvin's sermons and writings present a refreshing analysis of the providential institution of civil government and the various jurisdictions of life. His deep understanding of both the nature of man and the root of rebellion and revolution as well as the duties of rulers and citizens in the civil sphere and before God offers the modern reader a powerful and relevant exposition of Scripture's teachings on government and society.

God and the Civil Government is composed of excerpts from Calvin's sermons on Deuteronomy preached in Geneva in 1555 and 1556. The text has been translated from the published version *Sermons de M. Jean Calvin sur le v. livre de Moyse nommé Deuteronome* (Thomas Courteau, Geneva, 1567) and has been duly compared with Arthur Golding's English translation published in 1583 under the title *The Sermons of M. John Calvin upon the Fifth Book of Moses* (printed by Henry Middleton for Thomas Woodcocke, London).

Alongside these sermons, chapters six through eleven of this volume have been taken from Calvin's writing on the civil government in his *Institutes of the Christian Religion* (Henry Beveridge translation). Archaic words, phrases, and grammatical structures within the text have been updated for the sake of clarity and better understanding.

Unless otherwise noted, Scripture quotations are taken from the King James Version of the Holy Bible. Chapter breaks as well as headings within chapters have been added for ease of comprehension and do not appear in the original. Explanatory footnotes and Scripture references in brackets have also been added for clarification and do not appear in the original French text. Calvin's text has also been occasionally abridged.

CHAPTER ONE

The Weightiness
of Civil Office

*And I spake unto you at that time, saying, I am not able to
bear you myself alone: the LORD your God hath multiplied
you, and, behold, ye are this day as the stars of heaven for
multitude. (The LORD God of your fathers make you a
thousand times so many more as ye are, and bless you, as
he hath promised you!) How can I myself alone bear your
cumbrance, and your burden, and your strife? Take you
wise men, and understanding, and known among your
tribes, and I will make them rulers over you.*
Deuteronomy 1:9-13

Among the blessings that God poured out on the people
of Israel after delivering them from Egyptian bondage
is the fact that He took the governance of them into His
own hands. For, without this, what would become of mankind?
If we diligently consider this, we'll realize that there is less self-
government among men than among savage beasts. This is why
it is necessary for God to establish some order among them for
their proper government.

Now Moses reminds the people how God had been their
guide at all times. He wasn't merely content to rescue them from
that horrible captivity in which they had been held, but He also
established such a government and civil order among them that
nothing could prevent them from living at peace and walking in
perfect uprightness besides the wickedness dwelling within their

own hearts. It's the same as if Moses had said, "Do you see how greatly indebted to God you are? He has perfectly provided for you in every way. He has continually pitied you and has always preserved you safe and sound in every way."

Indeed, the remembrance of God's blessings should always incite and induce us to serve Him better. When we see that He has never failed us in any way, don't we have good reason to be as devoted to Him as possible and to completely dedicate ourselves to His obedience? For He shows us how precious we are to Him and what love He has for us and what care He has for us and our salvation when He provides for us in such a way.

Now, we must particularly note here that when God ordained a just civil order among us, and when He ordains men to uphold this order, this is an inestimable testimony of His goodness and love for us.

It's true that what Moses mentions here proceeded from the counsel of his father-in-law Jethro, as chapter eighteen of Exodus shows us (Ex. 18:17). And, though Jethro was a heathen man, yet God made use of him in this place. Thus we can see that God applies all things and all creatures for our benefit. Who would have thought that a man who had no acquaintance with the people of Israel (except for the fact that Moses had married a daughter of his house) would have come and given such counsel? But this is how God employs every creature for the benefit of His own people, just as I already mentioned.

HUMILITY, THE MARK OF A TRUE LEADER

Besides this, we must observe Moses' humility, for he didn't despise the admonishment given him by a man who hadn't been exalted to such a position as he had. Moses could have replied, "And who is this man? I have been chosen by God to lead and govern His Church and to be its head. I have proclaimed His Law in His name, and I have represented His majesty—so much so that it was given to me as a visible sign on my face as if I were an angel descended from heaven rather than a mortal man. I was separated from the company of mortal men for forty days, as if God had already carried me away to glory. And now will this unlearned man come forward and presume to instruct me?"

Moses could easily have spoken in this way, but he submitted himself to sound reason. Why? Because he knew that God distributes His gifts as He pleases, in such a way that the little can sometimes be of assistance to the greatest and most exalted. By this God desires to test the soberness and modesty of those whom He has raised to a position of authority. He tests them to see whether they will forget themselves or whether they will always be gentle and willing to learn and receive better counsel than what they themselves had considered, and whether they will humble themselves to receive this. This indeed is a true trial and proof of their obedience.

Considering the fact that Moses, who was the greatest among all the prophets of old, was perfectly willing to submit himself to the counsel of Jethro his father-in-law who didn't even know what the true religion was but had only tasted a drop of it in shadow as it were, how should we respond who have not even begun to approach the glory of Moses?

Thus, we must learn that, even though God may have filled us with His Spirit more fully than others, yet He didn't do this so that we could despise the advice and counsel of those who are below us. For this is how God desires us to be united and joined together with each other with a true bond—the greater condescending to the lower, and all agreeing together.

Moreover, as I just mentioned, even though Jethro was the instrument used to advise Moses, yet the counsel must be ascribed to God. He knew that this was suitable and proper for His people, for He didn't desire to leave them destitute in any way. This is why Moses speaks of it.

THE BURDEN OF GOVERNMENT

Now let's come to the words contained here.

First, he tells the people that he isn't able to bear them alone because they had increased greatly. He says, "ye are this day as the stars of heaven for multitude," and we know that they were more than 700,000 people. "How can I myself alone bear your cumbrance, and your burden, and your your strife? Take you wise men, and understanding, and known among your tribes."

First, when Moses declared that he wasn't able to bear the charge of the people, he shows that those who are elected to some degree of honor or some position of authority must not be like idols, without doing anything at all. To the contrary, they must labor in this position and must serve for the wellbeing of the entirety of the people, as if God had placed the burden of them upon their shoulders.

This is a teaching which is very good to note. For we see how much every man is given to ambition and how much each one desires to be esteemed and honored, and how they all aspire to greatness. Why is this? It's because we don't realize that God has raised us up in order that we might represent His person in the world. Now, this certainly can't be done without difficulties. Thus, the more honorable a charge or office is, the more painful and burdensome it will be. But men dream up lazy honors, and this dream carries them off into foolish—or rather insane—lusts, so much so that they seek nothing but their own reign and popularity and to be exalted as highly as they can—indeed, so much so that they often fall and break their own necks.

Secondly, we must also note that Moses said he wasn't able to bear so weighty a charge. This shows that he recognizes his own weakness. Or at least this shows that he was willing to walk in second place.

The next consideration that should correct our ambition and all foolish presumption within us is that, when we begin to diligently examine our own ability, then we will recognize that we would do much better to crawl under the earth than to covet this position of grandeur to lord it over our neighbors.

These are the two considerations that can abase our pride and foolish lusts for superiority. First, we much realize that, the higher a man is exalted, so much more also is he obligated both to God and to those over whom he is placed, for no preeminence exists without its accompanying burden—indeed, without its bondage or servitude, as I mentioned previously. That's the first point.

RECOGNIZING OUR INABILITY TO RULE

Secondly, we must also remember that we can't do anything of ourselves. Far from being able to bear such a great burden, we can't even have the smallest commission laid upon us without it pressing into our shoulders and making us bend under its weight. For our weakness is so great that anyone who considers himself honestly—without hypocrisy or delusive flattery—will see that he is scarcely strong enough to bear anything at all. Thus, if we properly consider our weakness, this knowledge will restrain us and serve as a bridle to prevent us from aspiring too high. For what will follow from this but utter confusion? What else could happen when men desire to be honored and yet don't desire to discharge their duty but instead make themselves like idols? Besides this, they don't even consider whether they possess sufficient ability for this.

Thirdly, we must note that, even though Moses recognized that the burden was too heavy for him, yet he didn't utterly renounce his calling or abandon the office God had committed to him. Instead, he asked for assistance and help, saying "Choose wise men."

This is well worth noting, for there are two vicious extremes that he might have resorted to. We've already condemned one of them, which is that men don't consider their own weakness but instead believe that it won't cost them anything to enjoy a position of authority. This causes them to have the recklessness and audacity to take on more than they are able to handle. They'll find themselves confounded in the end, but by that time it will be far too late.

Thus, it's a foolish presumption for men to forget themselves and attempt far too much because they have never considered their own inability. Such foolish endeavors will come to nothing but evil, for God will punish them for it.

Now there is also another evil extreme. This is when men become fainthearted because they recognize how weak they are. And, when God calls them to some office, they shrink back because they see that the task will be too difficult for them, and they attempt to cast off His yoke and flee the calling God has called them to. This is a sin we must beware of.

But there is a middle ground between these two: when we see that the difficulty surpasses our strength, we shoulder as much of it as we can bear, each according to his own measure. Then we set ourselves to pray, asking God to grant us the strength to fulfill whatever He demands of us. This is what we see displayed here in the example of Moses. He didn't abandon the government of the people, for by doing so he would have rebelled against God. (We see how He handled Jonah, for God found him even though he fled.) Thus, we mustn't refuse to obey God under pretence of our own weakness, even though the burdens He lays on us are most difficult to bear and even though we may tremble under their weight.

Whatever happens, we must hold to this rule: we must submit to God's calling and must follow Him wherever He pleases to call us. And, above all, we must call upon Him in order that He might supply all our needs and lacks. However, we must not attempt to take too much upon ourselves but must limit our charge to our abilities. If this advice were properly heeded, we wouldn't have so much confusion and such enormous chaos everywhere as we currently have.

If rulers nowadays considered the charge and burden they bear, do you think the whole world would be so troubled with wars, and do you think each of them would be striving with such zeal to snatch away someone else's land to enlarge his own dominion? Certainly not, for anyone who rules over a country or domain will find himself burdened quite enough with that, when he considers the office and duty he has both to God and his subjects.

Now here's a ruler with a country of two hundred leagues under him, and yet he attempts to subdue the entire world. Why? Because he hasn't considered the matter of this burden that Moses mentions here. Indeed, he here gives a rule—which is declared and pronounced by God Himself through Moses—to all those in any position of preeminence or authority, commanding that they must not make idols of themselves. They mustn't be content to sit over their subjects in pomp only, but they must also bear the burden of the people, which can't be accomplished without an honorable servitude, as we mentioned previously.

MAN'S INSATIABLE LUST FOR WEALTH

This rule also applies to private individuals. Everyone is always attempting to acquire more and more. And, when he has more than three times as much revenue as he can use for his own household, yet he still labors to snatch more and to join one piece to another. For no one asks himself, "How am I discharging my duty toward what God has given me? I have possessions in my hands. I have a family. I ought to occupy myself in instructing my wife, my children, and my servants in the fear of God. I ought to always be on the watch to see that nothing is done in my house that might offend God. Concerning my belongings, I ought to use them in a way that is in accordance with God's will. If I have an abundance beyond my needs, I should assist those who are in want and in need."

But no one considers this. Instead, those who have possessions are like a great abyss, swallowing up everything they can lay their hands on. They are concerned about nothing besides grasping more and more, and they give not a thought to those in need. They don't have a care in the world for anyone else—as long as they can make a profit. They pay no heed to God's honor but instead prefer to intoxicate themselves with the world and reign in it according to their own pleasures. In the meantime, they do nothing but rake together more and more, and they never consider that by doing so they are plunging themselves ever deeper and deeper into terrible damnation.

Therefore let us note the teaching given here by Moses, which is that each of us should consider—in the first place—that when it pleases God to put possessions into our hands or to elevate us to any position of authority, by doing this He binds us and measures us with a much stricter line, and we will have a much harder accounting to make to Him. Let us learn by this to hold ourselves within the bounds of our weak abilities when it so pleases God.

STRENGTH TO GOVERN COMES FROM GOD ALONE

Secondly, we must also be ever aware of our own weakness and must acknowledge that our ability is very small. And, if God chooses not to elevate us to a higher position, we must not envy those who are placed in such danger and who have such a weighty burden laid upon their shoulders. If they can't feel this burden, so much the worse for them. But, on our part (as I already said), we must be content that our Lord has left us seated on the ground, and we must not covet higher honors.

Yet we ought to have great compassion on those who bear such a difficult charge, and we ought to ask God to give them the fortitude for it and to strengthen them as they need it, for if God let them alone, they would fall and be utterly ruined.

Thirdly, if it pleases God to give us a commission in a position of authority, we must be prepared to obey Him, at least according to our ability. But we must not take too much upon ourselves, lest the ancient proverb be fulfilled in us: "He who grasps too much can scarcely maintain his grip." Instead, let us diligently offer ourselves to God, that He might rule us by His Spirit so that we each may fulfill our duties and employ ourselves according to our measure and ability and that we might all in common rely upon Him in all we do, that God might be served by us and that the fruits of our labor might benefit the people committed to our charge. This is what we should note here in summary.

CHAPTER TWO

A Citizen's Duty
in Electing Magistrates

*How can I myself alone bear your cumbrance, and your burden,
and your strife? Take you wise men, and understanding, and
known among your tribes, and I will make them rulers over you.
And ye answered me, and said, The thing which thou hast spoken
is good for us to do. So I took the chief of your tribes, wise men,
and known, and made them heads over you, captains over thousands, and captains over hundreds, and captains over fifties, and
captains over tens, and officers among your tribes.*
Deuteronomy 1:12-15

N ow we must also consider this saying of Moses: "So I
took the chief of your tribes, wise men, and known, and
made them heads over you, captains over thousands,
and captains over hundreds, and captains over fifties," as we'll
see. By this we are shown that, when we elect men to public office, we must choose them with discretion and must not flippantly pick whoever thrusts himself in first or make a choice
based on personal favoritism or good looks.

No, we must act in such a way that God may preside over
the election and that the men chosen are known to be suitable to
exercise the office to which they are called. We must specifically
observe what is recorded in the eighteenth chapter of Exodus
that we already mentioned, for Jethro said: "Provide out of all the
people able men, such as fear God, men of truth, hating covetousness" (Ex. 18:21). Who is it that speaks in this way? No more

than a poor heathen, as I already said. Yet God ruled his tongue in such a way that we could have no better instructor than he when it comes to choosing men to govern a people.

RULERS MUST BE MEN WHO FEAR GOD

First of all, he requires strong men—not effeminate—men who are able to bear such a charge. They must be zealous, courageous, and noble minded. Yet, since without the fear of God all other virtues a man may possess will be transformed into vices and wickedness, Jethro, who had never heard a single word of Holy Scripture, nevertheless clearly recognizes that it is impossible for a man to fulfill his duty in governing a people unless he fears God.

If a heathen man could speak like that, what shame ought we to have today when we possess less wisdom than he did? Yet we can easily see with our own eyes how things are run in the world. Do we consider, when we come to elect men to positions of civil justice, that the matter of greatest importance is that they must fear God? It's true that we will admit this, and even nature itself compels us to say that we must have wise and prudent men—as if we could have wisdom or prudence without the fear of God overruling everything! Jethro, in order to better express the fruits of this fear of God, adds: "men of justice and truth." It's as if he had said that a man could never be suitable to govern unless he were straightforward, not double minded, but ever walking with a pure conscience.

And, because bribes blind the eyes of the wise and pervert the justice of the righteous, he says that if we want to choose suitable men to rule, we must choose men who hate covetousness and must despise the goods of this world so that they have the willpower to pass them by when offered them. Thus, since such a lesson is taught us by a heathen, I ask you what shame it is on us who make a profession of being brought up in the Law of God and His Gospel, and who have our ears so full of it, and yet we are still novices to this teaching—or at least it is very poorly put into practice by us? Yet, despite our learning, if we do not put it to our profit, it will be stored up for our greater condemnation and will render us inexcusable.

THE SOLEMN DUTY OF CHOOSING MAGISTRATES

Thus, let us ponder well what Moses says here, exhorting the people to choose wise and understanding men, and men who have been tested. For, if we elected a man to office on hope alone, without any knowledge or experience of him, wouldn't this be a defiling of the throne of God and the seat of justice? God reserves to Himself the sovereignty over all men, as is also His due. Yet He wills to be served by mortal men as His ministers and officers. Therefore the seat of justice is, as it were, hallowed and sacred, as I'll show in the next lesson.

Now, some people elect a man haphazardly who has no idea what he should do or how to behave himself. They say, "We need to give him a chance and see what he can do. Once he's established in his office, he'll figure out how to run things." But would you take a farmhand or a shepherd into your house on hope alone, without him having any knowledge or understanding of what he was supposed to do? Will you set a man in God's seat of justice who has no knowledge? Will you choose a man without any previous experience to judge what kind of a man he is?

Thus, we must beware, particularly when God shows us this grace—indeed this privilege which isn't common to all people—to choose the men who govern us, lest we abuse such a good gift of God. If we don't, we will find ourselves suddenly deprived of this gift. This is why so many tyrannies have come upon the world and the liberty of so many peoples has been lost in such a way that they are no longer able to elect their own rulers. Indeed, rulers go so far as to buy and sell civil offices, and justice is so overturned that it's a horror to behold it. What is the reason for this? Isn't it the fact that the peoples who enjoyed some form of election have abused it? By their actions they prove that they are unworthy of possessing such a gift, so God has taken it and the honor He gave them away from them. For isn't it the same as willfully provoking God's wrath upon us when we despise Him by scorning the freedom of elections He gives us? When we should be choosing men to be His ministers of justice, instead we set our eyes on other things and waste our time in taverns—and, as if we acted out of spite and to mock God, we choose those who are the most dissolute and debauched to rule over us. Isn't this an utter perversion of all good order?

In short, it seems like we're attempting to cast God off His throne when we place His enemies and those who despise Him in His seat of justice and when we attempt nothing except to trample His majesty and name under our feet. When this is done, are we surprised if God sends such chaos into the world as we daily find there?

Thus, we ought to pay all the more attention to what is written here, for when God gives a people the liberty to choose their own officers, they must not abuse this but must instead use discretion and wisdom in choosing them. And, because we may often be deceived in our choice, we must flee to God and ask Him to give us wisdom and to govern us by His Holy Spirit, as if He had personally pointed out those whom we ought to elect. This is why I said that elections are never properly ruled and ordered unless God presides over them by His Holy Spirit.

Finally, Moses says, "I will make them rulers over you" (Deut. 1:13). He shows that God had given him this authority, but yet we see that he shared this authority with the people. His actions display what we already noted, that he didn't ascribe to himself any undue power but that he recognized and acknowledged that God appointed him to labor for the common good.

Thus Moses had authority and clearly recognized that God willed for him to be placed above the rest of the people. But yet he didn't abuse his office, but instead he imparted it to the people. It's as if he said, "I will simply show you how you ought to lead yourselves, and yet I will take the pains on myself and will instead give the honor to you." This same mindset ought to exist in all good magistrates and governors—that is, that they might retain the authority required of them, for this is the reason why God has elevated them to that office. Yet, no matter what else they do, they must not seek their own profit but must labor to prepare themselves as much as possible to properly fulfill their duty, always upholding the main charge laid upon them by God.

CHAPTER THREE

A Judge's Duty Before God

*And I charged your judges at that time, saying, Hear
the causes between your brethren, and judge righteously
between every man and his brother, and the stranger that
is with him. Ye shall not respect persons in judgment; but
ye shall hear the small as well as the great; ye shall not be
afraid of the face of man; for the judgment is God's.*
Deuteronomy 1:16-18

We saw previously the warning Moses gave concerning choosing suitable men to govern the people. For, as I mentioned, if we elected judges at random, we would profane and defile God's throne. Thus we must use wisdom and discretion.

But here Moses adds something that we ought to note well. For, even though he stipulated that those who were elected must be men who fear God and who were endowed with particular gifts or abilities, yet he doesn't cease to show them what their office will entail and warn them what they must do in the execution of it. By this we see that even the wisest still need to be taught, and the most upright and righteous still need to be warned and admonished.

Therefore, if God has already set us in the good way and has already given us the gifts of His Holy Spirit, yet we mustn't think that we no longer need to be instructed. For we must always be guided—even to the very end—for we know that we will never attain perfection in this world or as long as we are in this sinful flesh and dwell here below. Therefore, those whom God has honored by elevating them to this position and this degree of honor must recognize that they still need to be told their duty and must still be incited to discharge themselves accordingly.

THE DUTY OF JUDGES

Now let's move on to what is written here. In the first place, Moses instructs judges and governors to "Hear the causes." By this he means that they must be attentive and diligent to know the rights of every person. For, if a judge doesn't condescend to hear, how will he execute his office? We know that, even when men take great pains to judge rightly, yet because of their own frailty and weakness, they might fail to do so. And, if they are negligent besides, everything will most certainly devolve into chaos and confusion. Therefore Moses had good reason to particularly exhort judges to hear and understand properly.

Then he expressly says, "between your brethren, . . . and the stranger." It's as if he said that every person must be permitted to offer his own defense. Even though this examination often produces favor or hatred, yet a judge must diligently execute his office, forgetting all that might cause him to favor either one side or the other. And, since foreigners didn't have any support or assistance, the judge must provide for this. And, though he can expect no reward or thanks from such a person, yet he still must not fail to execute his office and do right, for this service is pleasing to God. Even though it receives such a poor reward from men, yet God is quite powerful enough to repay him.

Thus, all those who hold the office of justices have their lesson here set down in writing: they must uphold right and justice for all those who are committed to their charge. For, as I already mentioned, the state of justice is an honorable and righteous service. Those who are elevated to such a position mustn't dominate over their subjects or trample them underfoot or even fail to consider their wellbeing. To the contrary, they are bound and obligated to them, and live (in a way) a life of servitude. For God didn't create nations to satisfy a few men's pleasures and allow the entire race of mankind to be subject to them. But He created them for the common good of all. Thus, if rulers don't realize that they are bound by the will of God and the order of nature to those committed to their care, they must certainly render an account to God for having abused His grace and the honor that He has shown them. This is what we must note here.

RULERS ARE BOUND TO GOD AND MUST GIVE AN ACCOUNT TO HIM

Now we must also note that, if rulers are bound to the people under them in this way, how much more are they bound and obligated to God! If they were sitting in judgment over a matter in which a man had been defrauded of five cents—or even less—if justice is not rendered to him, we see what is said here.

Now, if God's name is blasphemed and if His honor is obscured when wicked and dishonest matters are countenanced and when those who sit in the seat of justice and who bear the sword in hand don't use it to resist evil and to correct the wrongs done against God, will they be excused? For, if they allow a wronged man to be defrauded of even a single penny, they will stand guilty before God. And it's an even greater matter when it concerns the majesty of God and His honor and worship.

Thus, we must note that if magistrates are bound to render justice to everyone in even the smallest matters or matters of little importance, they must labor to uphold the honor of God with much greater zeal in comparison to this. Above all, when it's a question concerning the reign of our Lord Jesus Christ, the entire world isn't worthy to be compared with Him, for the glory of God shines forth here. Thus we must also take note of this in this passage.

CHAPTER FOUR

The Danger of Fearing Men

*Ye shall not respect persons in judgment; but ye shall hear
the small as well as the great; ye shall not be afraid of the
face of man; for the judgment is God's.*
Deuteronomy 1:17

Since we are always prone to fear men in such a way that we experience strong and fierce temptations to hinder us from executing our duty, Moses expressly warns judges not to fear men. Why? Because "the judgment is God's" (Deut. 1:17). Here is a verse well worth studying.

I already mentioned what experience shows all too clearly, which is that men of good and sound judgment nevertheless fail to execute their office properly because of their timidity.

For example, here's a man in a seat of justice. He isn't a wicked man, and he truly desires to order all things well. He is grieved when he sees any wrongdoing and would rejoice if every person would govern themselves properly or if some suitable correction was given when someone committed a crime. Yet, at the same time, he also sees the complainers and the malcontents, so he asks himself:

"Why should I do this? If I judge rightly, everyone will get angry at me. That man has relatives and friends who could take their revenge on me if I punish him. And, because iniquity runs rampant everywhere and the wicked do as they please and are multiplying everywhere, I would have to declare war on the entire world if I attempted to faithfully execute my duty. I couldn't merely set myself against only two or three because there are so many criminals, and everyone resists justice."

Thus, those who fear something other than God and who desire to execute righteousness and justice in the seat of judgment are hindered by their timidity. If they consider the persons of men, they will surely be shaken and knocked over. Why is this?

It's because they aren't standing on this foundation that Moses sets down here: "the judgment is God's." They don't realize the grave dishonor and reproach they render to God when they have a greater consideration for men than for Him. For whoever turns aside from his duty out of fear has a higher view of man than of God.

Why? A judge must realize and consider that God has established him in the office he holds. He must not act the part of a mere creature, for whoever serves in the place of justice is seated on the throne of God and is like His lieutenant.[1] Thus, a judge must pay careful consideration to this. If he doesn't, he has already forgotten God, whom he is bound to serve.

This would be the same as if a man were hired to serve his master and yet didn't know whether or not there was anyone in the house to serve. Instead, he contents himself with singing, playing, eating and drinking at all hours, and sleeping whenever he likes, without ever giving any consideration for his master. Wouldn't such a man who so forgets his master and his labor deserve to be publicly shamed and condemned? Now, if judges won't consider this and won't consider from whom they have received their office and dignity, this is base ingratitude—indeed, and is absolute stupidity and villainous beastliness.

On the other hand, if judges recognize that God has elevated them to their office and yet they still allow themselves to be prevented from executing their office out of fear of men and are thus restrained from doing what they know to be their duty because men are against them, what do they offer to God? What opinion do they hold of His power and virtue? Yet God here teaches them their lesson and promises to assist them and be their defender. Thus, shouldn't they take His invincible power as

---

[1] French *lieutenant*, that is, a representative, someone standing in the place of another.

their shield, and shouldn't they be prepared to enter battle even if the entire world is against them?

Isn't God strong enough to assist and aid them in this if they place their trust in Him and rest on Him, drawing from this a steadfastness and courage to walk in the path of justice and right? Otherwise, if they are moved by such temptations to turn aside form their duty, they must realize that by their actions they seek to strip God's power from Him. Thus we can clearly see that this passage gives us very profitable instruction.

WE MUST NOT BELITTLE GOD

But yet we must also note that this not only applies to those in authority but also to all in general. For no comparison can be made between God and mortal men. Why is this? Because nothing deceives us more than when we ascribe too much to men by making God smaller or by seeking to abolish His majesty. As soon as some person stands before us, suddenly God is nothing in comparison to him. And, if we placed the two in a balance, it would seem as if He didn't bear the weight of a feather while men always carry their full weight toward us.

It's true that if we begin to compare a person against ourselves, we make much less of him, for we all know how to make much of ourselves. Or, if we compare one person with another, whoever is more to our liking will possess the greater appearance and will be able to reveal the despicability of the opposite party. Someone will say, "What is he? He's a nobody!" Why is this? We think more of the other person.

Thus we know quite well enough how to despise men. But when we come to God, we attempt to cast Him down entirely and must elevate men into His position of authority. Here you can see our wickedness and perversity on display.

Thus, how much greater heed should we pay to this verse that shows us that, when God is before us, we must never consider men, for this is far too grave a sacrilege and treason against Him when man—or any creature—is held in such great esteem that God's rights are obscured or we seek to snatch His preroga-tives from Him. Yet we see that this is far too common, and it hinders us from serving God as we ought.

It's true that we are each led astray by our own wicked lusts. Even if there were nothing else that sought to hinder us besides this, we have enough within us to lead us astray. And our nature is so wicked that we can't set ourselves to do go as we ought.

LIVING IN FEAR OF MEN'S DISAPPROVAL

Yet there's still another evil in the fact that when a man comes before us, we're easily overcome.

"I know I must fulfill my duty," we say, "but what can I do? If I execute my duty, I bring upon myself this man's hatred."

We see nowadays that you can't possibly please anyone without howling with the wolves (as they say) or without doing exactly what the world is doing and without following the herd.

Or, as another example, my neighbor comes to me. I'll find myself at odds with him for the rest of my life if I don't con-form to his expectations. He's my friend, so I ought to bear with him, shouldn't I? Thus we see how debauchery and all other evils come into play, for every person attempts to please his neighbor, and his neighbor despises God. For, when fornication, drunken-ness, and other wickedness reign, each person is infected by the example of his neighbor, and everyone catches the disease from someone else. What is the cause of all this? It's the fact that we think too highly of people and don't recognize that we ought to reject both small and great and instead earnestly bend our ener-gies to conform ourselves to the will of God.

Thus, let us diligently meditate upon this teaching which is here given not only to judges but also to all of us in general. Since the judgment is God's, we must never be moved by the face of men, no matter who they may be, but we must give God His preeminence and must cast down all concern for the persons of men. If people frighten us, we must resist this fear and must not commit the sin of snatching away what belongs to God to give it to His creatures. Thus we see what we must learn from this.

CHAPTER FIVE

God, the Sovereign Ruler
Over All Rulers

Ye shall not respect persons in judgment; but ye shall hear
the small as well as the great; ye shall not be afraid of the
face of man; for the judgment is God's.
Deuteronomy 1:17

Secondly, when it's said that "the judgment is God's," this text carries a very good lesson with it. It's true that Moses speaks here of the office that judges and magistrates hold. It's as if he said that they mustn't consider this as their personal possession or as their own inheritance, but only as a simple office that God has placed them in. And, by placing them in such a position of honor, He in no way abdicated His own majesty. He never said, "My creatures can rule with absolute power, and I won't hold any position anymore."

Thus, when God elevated these men to their office, He in no way diminished His own position, for He always possesses sovereign dominion over all men, and they are nothing more than instruments of His power. Consequently, they must serve Him and must submit all things to Him. If this teaching were better taught and known, kings and rulers wouldn't rule with such tyranny today as they do, and we would certainly see a greater humility in all places than what we currently see. For those who are placed in positions of honor consider that the world was made for them. Therefore they reject all admonitions and all laws and statutes, and they break the yoke from off their necks as if they lived in perfect freedom and considered God to be nonexistent.

Yet in this verse Moses shows that the authority and position of kings and rulers must never diminish God's authority, but instead His glory ought always to remain in its fullness unabated. Why is this? What are rulers of the world except officers of God appointed so that, through them, He might be obeyed and all might render homage to Him, and that the king as the highest among his subjects must give an example to the lowest?

Thus, since the judgment is God's, those who pervert the order of civil government when they are called to do their duty will receive a double condemnation. Therefore kings and rulers—and all those in any position of justice—will have a very difficult account to render to God. For, if they fail in their duty, they aren't only obligated to men and haven't only offended the creatures, but they've also transgressed the majesty of God and have desecrated His throne. Why is this? It's because judgment belongs to Him, and He has reserved it to Himself.

Thus, we must carefully note this teaching where he says, "the judgment is God's." That is, all authority and power that men possess in whatever position they enjoy should never diminish God's preeminence but should instead uphold and promote it. What then are all positions of honor and dignity and all high offices in this world? They're nothing more than a means by which God reigns among us and by which we each learn to humble ourselves under Him and acknowledge that we must obey Him in all things and in all cases.

What then is the duty of kings, emperors, and magistrates? They must see that God is exalted and magnified as He ought to be and that all their subjects render homage to Him. And they, as leaders, must show them the way.

Further, what is the duty of teachers and fathers and all those who hold authority in these positions in the family? They must each consider how God has honored them in their own position.

A man who has children must consider, "You stand in

the place of God in your role as a father." But yet God has not abdicated His own honor to vest it in this man. How does this work? "He is still the Father of both myself and my children," he says. "I must endeavor to bring all into obedience to Him."

And what of a master? Does he say, "This position of authority is mine"? No. "God is the One who has graciously raised me to this position, even though I don't deserve it. It pleased Him to give me people to govern. Yet it is He who must rule me and all those under my authority." This, I say, is how we must put this teaching into practice.

Civil Government is Ordained by God

Let every soul be subject unto the higher powers. For there is no power but of God: the powers that be are ordained of God. Whosoever therefore resisteth the power, resisteth the ordinance of God: and they that resist shall receive to themselves damnation. For rulers are not a terror to good works, but to the evil. Wilt thou then not be afraid of the power? do that which is good, and thou shalt have praise of the same: for he is the minister of God to thee for good.
Romans 13:1-4

With regard to the office of magistrates, the Lord has not only declared that He approves and is pleased with it, but He has also strongly recommended it to us by the very honorable titles He has conferred upon it. To mention a few:

When those who bear the office of magistrate are called gods, let no one suppose that there is little weight in that title. By this we are shown that they have a commission from God, that they are invested with divine authority, and, in fact, that they represent the person of God, whose representatives they are. This is not a quibble of mine but is the interpretation of Christ. "If Scripture," says He, "called them gods, to whom the word of God came." What does this mean but that the business was committed to them by God? He appointed them to serve Him in their office, and (as Moses and Jehoshaphat said to the judges whom they were appointing over each of the cities of Judah) to exercise judgment, not for man, but for God.

Wisdom affirms the same thing by the mouth of Solomon, saying: "By me kings reign, and princes decree justice. By me princes rule, and nobles, even all the judges of the earth" (Prov. 3:15-16). For this is the same as if it were said that human perversity isn't the reason why supreme power on earth is lodged in kings and other governors, but it is because of divine providence and the holy decree of Him to whom it has seemed good so to govern the affairs of men, since He is present and also presides in enacting laws and exercising judicial equity.

Paul also plainly teaches this when he lists offices of ruling among the gifts of God which, distributed variously according to the measure of grace, ought to be employed by the servants of Christ for the edification of the Church (Rom. 12:8). In that place, however, he is properly speaking of the council of sober men who were appointed in the early Church to take charge of public discipline. In the epistle to the Corinthians, this office is called "governments" (1 Cor. 12:28). Still, as we see that civil power has the same end in view, there can be no doubt that he is recommending every kind of just government.

Paul speaks much more clearly when he comes to a detailed discussion of the subject. For he says that "there is no power but of God: the powers that be are ordained of God." Thus, rulers are the ministers of God, "not a terror to good works, but to the evil" (Rom. 13:1-3).

To this we may add the examples of saints, some of whom held the offices of kings, as David, Josiah, and Hezekiah; others of governors, as Joseph and Daniel; others of civil magistrates among a free people, as Moses, Joshua, and the Judges. Their functions were expressly approved by the Lord. Therefore no man can doubt that civil authority is, in the sight of God, not only sacred and lawful, but the *most* sacred and by far the most honorable of all stations in mortal life.

THOSE WHO DENY THE LEGITIMACY OF CIVIL GOVERNMENT

Those who desire to introduce anarchy would object that, though in former times kings and judges ruled over ignorant and unlearned people, yet in the present day, this servile mode of governing does not at all agree with the perfection which Christ brought with His gospel. By this they betray not only their ignorance but also their devilish pride, for they arrogantly ascribe to themselves a perfection of which not even a hundredth part is seen in them.

But, be that as it may, it's easy to refute them. For, when David says, "Be wise now therefore, O ye kings: be instructed, ye judges of the earth," and "Kiss the Son, lest he be angry," he doesn't order these rulers to lay aside their authority and return to private life (Ps. 2:10-12). Instead, he commands them to subject the power they hold to Christ, that He may rule over all.

In the same way, when Isaiah predicts of the Church, "Kings shall be thy nursing fathers, and their queens thy nursing mothers" (Isa. 49:23), he doesn't tell them to abdicate their authority. Instead, he gives them the honorable titles of patrons of the pious worshippers of God, for this prophecy refers to the coming of Christ. I intentionally omit many passages which occur throughout Scripture (and especially in the psalms) in which the due authority of all rulers is asserted. The most well-known passage of all is that in which Paul, when admonishing Timothy that prayers should be offered up in the public assembly for kings, adds the reason why: "that we may lead a quiet and peaceable life in all godliness and honesty" (1 Tim. 2:2). In these words, he commends the condition of the Church to the protection and guardianship of the civil government.

MAGISTRATES MUST FAITHFULLY EXECUTE THEIR OFFICE AS GOD'S REPRESENTATIVES

This consideration ought to be constantly present in the minds of magistrates, for it will help to create a strong incentive to the discharge of their duty. It will also give them extraordinary consolation by smoothing the difficulties of their office, which are certainly numerous and weighty. What zeal for integrity, prudence, meekness, self-control, and innocence ought to sway those who know that they have been appointed ministers of divine justice! How will they dare to allow iniquity to enter into their courts of justice when they are told that this is the throne of the living God? How will they dare to pronounce an unjust sentence with their mouth when they understand that it is an ordained organ of divine truth? How could they in good conscience sign ungodly decrees with a hand that they know has been appointed to write the acts of God?

In short, if they remember that they are the representatives of God, they must watch with all care, diligence, and industry, so that they may exhibit in themselves a kind of image of divine providence, guardianship, goodness, benevolence, and justice. And let them constantly keep this additional thought in view, that if a curse is pronounced on him who "doeth the work of the Lord deceitfully," a much heavier curse will fall on him who deals deceitfully in a righteous calling.

Therefore, when Moses and Jehoshaphat urged their judges to the discharge of their duty, they had nothing by which they could more powerfully stimulate their minds than the consideration we've already referred to: "Take heed what ye do: for ye judge not for man, but for the Lord, who is with you in the judgment. Wherefore now let the fear of the Lord be upon you; take heed and do it: for there is no iniquity with the Lord our God, nor respect of persons, nor taking of gifts" (2 Chron. 19:6-7, compared with Deut. 1:16-18).

And in another passage it is said, "God standeth in the congregation of the mighty; he judgeth among the gods" (Ps. 82:1; Isa. 3:14). This is written to spur them on to their duty, for they hear that they are ambassadors of God, to whom they must one day render an account of the authority committed to them. This admonition certainly ought to have the greatest effect upon them. For, if they sin in any way at all, not only is injury done to the men whom they wickedly sin against, but they also insult God Himself, whose sacred tribunals they defile.

On the other hand, they have an admirable source of comfort when they reflect that they are not engaged in a profane calling unworthy of a servant of God but are instead in a most sacred office, for they are the ambassadors of God.

GOD HAS APPOINTED ALL TYPES OF CIVIL GOVERNMENT

Some refuse to be persuaded by all these passages of Scripture. They speak against this sacred ministry as if it were something abhorrent to religion and Christian godliness. But when they do this, aren't they attacking God Himself, who is most certainly insulted when His servants are disgraced? These men not only speak evil of dignities, but they don't even want God to reign over them (1 Sam. 7:7). For, if this was truly said of the people of Israel when they refused the authority of Samuel, how can it be less truly said in the present day of those who allow themselves to break loose against all the authority established by God?

But they will declare that when our Lord said to His disciples, "The kings of the Gentiles exercise lordship over them; and they that exercise authority upon them are called benefactors. But ye shall not be so: but he that is greatest among you, let him be as the younger; and he that is chief, as he that doth serve," He in this way prohibited all Christians from becoming kings or governors (Luke 22:25-26). Such sly interpreters they are! A dispute had arisen among the disciples as to which of them would be greatest. To suppress this vain ambition, our Lord taught them that their ministry was not like the power and authority of earthly rulers, among whom one greatly surpasses another. I ask you, how can this be used to disparage royal authority? To the contrary, what does it prove at all except that the office of civil government is not the same as the apostolic ministry?

Besides, though different forms exist in civil offices, yet there is no difference in the fact that they must all be received by us as ordinances of God. For Paul includes all together when he says that "there is no power but of God," and even the least pleasing of all was honored with the highest testimonial—I mean the power of one. When a single person rules, everyone else is in subjection to that person. This form of government was formerly disliked by heroic and more excellent natures, but Scripture expressly affirms that even this is given by divine wisdom. It is by God's wisdom that "kings reign." We are also specifically commanded "to honour the king" (1 Pet. 2:17).

CHAPTER SEVEN

Various Forms of Civil Government

It would certainly be a very useless occupation for private individuals to discuss what would be the best form of civil government in the place where they live, for these deliberations can't have any influence in determining any public matter. Also, the matter itself couldn't be defined absolutely without rashness, since the nature of the discussion depends on circumstances. And if you compare different states with each other, without regard to circumstances, it isn't easy to determine which of these has the advantage in point of use, for they are so equal concerning the terms on which they meet.

Monarchy is prone to tyranny. But, in an aristocracy, the tendency is not less to the faction of a few. In democracy, there is the strongest tendency to revolution. When these three forms of government that the philosophers discuss are considered in themselves, I, for my part, am far from denying that the form which greatly surpasses the others is aristocracy, either pure or modified by popular government. It isn't the best in itself, but simply because it very rarely happens that kings so rule themselves as never to dissent from what is just and right, or are possessed of so much wisdom and prudence as always to see correctly. Owing, therefore, to the vices or defects of men, it is safer and more tolerable when several bear rule, that they may thus mutually assist, instruct, and admonish each other. And, if any one them is tempted to go too far, the others are censors and masters to curb his excess.

This has already been proved by experience and

confirmed also by the authority of the Lord Himself when He established an aristocracy bordering on popular government among the Israelites. He kept them under that as the best form until He showed them a picture of the Messiah in David. And, as I willingly admit that there is no kind of government happier than where liberty is set down with suitable moderation and is duly constituted so as to be long-lasting, so I consider those very happy who are permitted to enjoy that form of government. I admit that they do nothing contrary to their duty when they strenuously and constantly labor to preserve and maintain such an order.

Indeed, even magistrates ought to do their utmost to prevent liberty from being curtailed or violated. They have been appointed guardians of this same liberty. If they are negligent or careless in this, they are despicable traitors to their office and their country.

But, if those to whom the Lord has assigned one form of government take it upon themselves to long for a change, such a wish would not only be foolish and superfluous but very dangerous. If you fix your eyes not on one state alone but look around the world, or at least direct your view to regions widely separated from each other, you will perceive that divine providence has good reason for causing different countries to be governed by different forms of government. For, just as elements of unequal temperature adhere together, so in different regions a similar inequality in the form of government is best. All this, however, is said unnecessarily to those to whom the will of God is a sufficient reason. For, if it has pleased Him to appoint kings over kingdoms, and senates or governors over free states, whichever form He has appointed in the places in which we live, it is our duty to obey and submit to it.

CHAPTER EIGHT

The Law by Which Magistrates Must Rule

L et me mention in passing what the nature of a magistrate's duty is, as described by the Word of God, and the things in which it consists. Scripture teaches us that their duty extends to both tables of the law. Even secular writers agree with this, for no one has written on the duty of magistrates, the enacting of laws, and the commonwealth without beginning with religion and divine worship. Thus all have agreed that no civil government can be successfully established unless piety is its first care and unless those laws are ridiculous which disregard the rights of God and only have a consideration for men.

Thus, since religion holds the first place even among philosophers, and since the same thing has always been observed with the universal consent of nations, Christian rulers and magistrates ought to be ashamed of their cowardice if they refuse to make this their care. We have already shown that this office is specially assigned them by God. And indeed it is right that they should exert themselves to assert and defend the honor of Him whose representatives they are, and by whose favor they rule.

Thus, in Scripture holy kings are particularly praised for restoring the worship of God when it has been corrupted or overthrown, or for taking care that religion flourished under them in purity and safety. On the other hand, sacred history sets down anarchy as a wicked sin when it states that there was no king in Israel and, therefore, everyone did as he pleased (Judg. 21:25). This rebukes the folly of those who would neglect the care of divine things and devote themselves merely to the administration of justice among men—as if God had appointed rulers in His own name to decide earthly controversies and yet omitted what was of far greater importance, His own pure worship as prescribed by His law. Such views are adopted by rebellious men who, in their eagerness to make all kinds of innovations with impunity, desire to abolish all the vindicators of violated piety.

In regard to the second table of the law, Jeremiah addresses rulers, "Thus saith the Lord, Execute ye judgment and righteousness, and deliver the spoiled out of the hand of the oppressor: and do no wrong, do no violence to the stranger, the fatherless, nor the widow, neither shed innocent blood" (Jer. 22:3).

The exhortation in Psalms speaks the same way: "Defend the poor and fatherless; do justice to the afflicted and needy. Deliver the poor and needy; rid them out of the hand of the wicked" (Ps. 82:3-4).

Moses also declared to the rulers whom he had substituted for himself, "Hear the causes between your brethren, and judge righteously between every man and his brother, and the stranger that is with him. Ye shall not respect persons in judgment; but ye shall hear the small as well as the great: ye shall not be afraid of the face of man, for the judgment is God's" (Deut. 1:16).

I won't touch on such passages as these, "He shall not multiply horses to himself, nor cause the people to return to Egypt;" "neither shall he multiply wives to himself; neither shall he greatly multiply to himself silver and gold;" "he shall write him a copy of this law in a book;" "and it shall be with him, and he shall read therein all the days of his life, that he may learn to fear the Lord his God;" "that his heart be not lifted up above his brethren" (Deut. 17:16-20).

In explaining the duties of magistrates here, my exposition is intended not so much for the instruction of magistrates themselves as to teach others why there are magistrates, and why they have been appointed by God. We say, therefore, that they are the ordained guardians and vindicators of public innocence, modesty, honor, and tranquility, so that their only concern should be to provide for the common peace and safety. Of these things David declares that he will set an example when he ascended to the throne. "A froward heart shall depart from me: I will not know a wicked person. Whoso privily slandereth his neighbour, him will I cut off: him that hath an high look and a proud heart will not I suffer. Mine eyes shall be upon the faithful of the land, that they may dwell with me: he that walketh in a perfect way, he shall serve me" (Ps. 101:4-6).

But, since rulers can't do this unless they protect the good from the injuries of the wicked and unless they give aid and protection to the oppressed, they are armed with power to curb blatant evildoers and criminals, by whose misconduct the public tranquility is disturbed or harassed. For we have full experience of the truth of Solon's saying, that all public matters depend on reward and punishment; and where these are lacking, the whole discipline of the nation totters and falls to pieces. For, in the minds of many, the love of justice and equity grows cold if due honor isn't paid to virtue. And the licentiousness of the wicked can't be restrained without strict discipline and the infliction of punishment.

These two things are included by the prophet when he commands kings and other rulers to execute "judgment and righteousness" (Jer. 21:12; 22:3). It is righteousness (or justice) to take charge of the innocent, to defend and avenge them, and to set them free. It is judgment to withstand the audacity of the wicked, to repress their violence, and to punish their faults.

CHAPTER NINE

Honor and Obedience

Honour all men. Love the brotherhood. Fear God.
Honour the king.
1 Peter 2:17

HONORING THOSE IN AUTHORITY

The first duty of subjects towards their rulers is to view their office with great honor, recognizing it as a delegated jurisdiction from God, and on that account receiving and reverencing them as the ministers and ambassadors of God. For you will find some who are very obedient to magistrates and who don't desire to abolish the role of magistrates because they know this is necessary for the public good, and yet they are of the opinion that magistrates are a kind of necessary evil. But Peter requires something more of us when he says, "Honour the king" (1 Pet. 2:17). Solomon does the same when he says, "My son, fear thou the Lord and the king" (Prov. 24:21). For, by the term *honor,* Peter means a sincere and candid esteem, and Solomon, by joining the king with God, shows that he is invested with a kind of holy reverence and dignity.

We also have the remarkable admonition from Paul: "Be subject not only for wrath, but also for conscience sake" (Rom. 13:5). By this he means that subjects, in submitting to rulers and governors, are not to be influenced merely by fear (like people who submit to an armed enemy because they know they will suffer if they resist), but because this obedience is rendered to God Himself since the ruler's power comes from God.

I don't mean that men can exercise their folly, cowardice, cruelty, or wicked or debauched morals under cover of this authority and thus acquire praise for vice instead of virtue. But I mean that the office itself is deserving of honor and reverence and that we ought to esteem and hold in reverence those who rule.

OBEDIENCE TO AUTHORITIES

From this follows a second thing, which is that we must willingly show our obedience to them by obeying their commands; or by paying taxes; or by undertaking public offices and burdens which relate to the common defense; or in executing any other orders. "Let every soul," says Paul, "be subject unto the higher powers." "Whosoever, therefore, resisteth the power, resisteth the ordinance of God" (Rom. 13:1-2). Writing to Titus, he says, "Put them in mind to be subject to principalities and powers, to obey magistrates, to be ready to every good work" (Tit. 3:1). Peter also says, "Submit yourselves to every ordinance of man for the Lord's sake: whether it be to the king, as supreme; or unto governors, as unto them that are sent by him for the punishment of evildoers, and for the praise of them that do well" (1 Pet. 2:13-14).

Also, to prove that we aren't merely pretending to obey but are instead sincerely and willingly subject to them, Paul adds that we must pray to God for the safety and prosperity of those under whom we live. "I exhort, therefore," says he, "that, first of all, supplications, prayers, intercessions, and giving of thanks, be made for all men; for kings, and for all that are in authority: that we may lead a quiet and peaceable life in all godliness and honesty" (1 Tim. 2:1-2).

Let no man here deceive himself, since we cannot resist the magistrate without resisting God. For, though we may think that we can despise an unarmed magistrate with impunity, yet God is armed, and He will powerfully avenge this contempt.

Under this obedience, I include the restraint which private individuals ought to impose on themselves in public, not interfering with public business or rashly encroaching on the jurisdiction of the magistrate or attempting anything at all of a public nature. If it is proper that anything in a public ordinance should be corrected, let them not act tumultuously or put their hands to a work where they ought to admit that their hands are tied, but let them leave it to the judgment of the magistrate, whose hand alone is free here.

My meaning is, let them not dare to do it without being commissioned to do so. For, when the command of the magistrate is given, then they too are invested with public authority. For, according to the common saying, the eyes and ears of the ruler are his counselors. So also we wouldn't be amiss in saying that those who, by his command, have the charge of managing affairs, are his hands.

OBEDIENCE MUST BE RENDERED EVEN TO UNJUST CIVIL AUTHORITIES

But, since until now we've only described a magistrate who is truly what he ought to be—that is, the father of his country and the shepherd of the people, the guardian of peace, the president of justice, and the vindicator of innocence, we would justly consider a person insane if he disapproved of such authority.

And, since in almost all ages we see that some rulers become careless about all the duties they ought to execute and instead live without a care in luxurious sloth; and others, bent on their own interest, wickedly prostitute all rights, privileges, judgments, and enactments; others pillage poor people of their money and afterwards squander it in insane gifts; others act as mere robbers, pillaging houses, violating women, and murdering the innocent—because of these abuses, many cannot be persuaded to acknowledge such persons as rulers whom they are bound to obey (as far as their commands are lawful). For, in this unworthy conduct and these horrible atrocities so alien not only to the duty of a magistrate but also of a human, they can't see any vestige of the image of God which ought to be conspicuous in a magistrate.

Because they can't discern a vestige of the minister of God who was appointed to be a praise to the good and a terror to the evil, they cannot acknowledge the ruler whose dignity and authority Scripture commends to us. And, undoubtedly, the natural feeling of the human mind has always been more prone to treat tyrants with hatred and scorn rather than to honor just kings with love and reverence.

WICKED RULERS ARE A JUDGMENT FROM GOD

But, if we examine the Word of God, it will lead us farther and will show that we are subject not only to the authority of rulers who honestly and faithfully perform their duty toward us but to all rulers, no matter how they have become our rulers, even if they in no way fulfill their duty as rulers. For, though the Lord declares that a ruler who upholds the public peace is the highest gift of His blessing, and though He appoints each ruler to their proper sphere, yet at the same time He declares that—no matter what kind of ruler they are—they derive their power from none but Him.

Those indeed who rule for the public good are true examples and patterns of His beneficence, while those who rule unjustly and tyrannically are raised up by Him to punish the people for their iniquity. Still, He has given to both alike that sacred majesty with which He has invested lawful power.

Before going any further, I must add some clear passages that deal with this. We don't need to prove that a wicked king is a mark of the Lord's anger, since I presume no one will deny that, and since this is no less true of a king than of a robber who plunders your goods, an adulterer who defiles your bed, and an assassin who aims at your life, since all such calamities are classed by Scripture among the curses of God.

But let us insist at greater length in proving what is not so easily seen and agreed to by men, which is that even an individual of the worst character and one most unworthy of all honor, if he is invested with public authority, receives that illustrious divine power which the Lord has by His Word bestowed on the ministers of His justice and judgment. Thus, as far as public obedience is concerned, we must hold such a man in the same honor and reverence as the best of kings.

CHAPTER TEN

Lessons From Scripture Concerning Tyrants

And David said to Abishai, Destroy him not: for who can stretch forth his hand against the LORD's anointed, and be guiltless? David said furthermore, As the LORD liveth, the LORD shall smite him; or his day shall come to die; or he shall descend into battle, and perish. The LORD forbid that I should stretch forth mine hand against the LORD's anointed.

1 Samuel 26:9-11

irst, let the reader carefully observe that divine providence which—with good reason—is so often set before us in Scripture, and that particular act of distributing kingdoms and setting up as kings whoever He pleases. In Daniel it is said, "He changeth the times and the seasons: he removeth kings, and setteth up kings" (Dan. 2:21, 37). Again, "That the living may know that the Most High ruleth in the kingdom of men, and giveth it to whomsoever he will" (Dan. 4:17, 25).

Similar words occur throughout Scripture, but they abound particularly in the prophetical books. We are well aware of what kind of king Nebuchadnezzar was, who laid siege to Jerusalem. He was an active invader and devastator of other countries. Yet the Lord declares in Ezekiel that He had given him the land of Egypt as his reward for the devastation which he had committed. Daniel also said to him, "Thou, O king, art a king of kings: for the God of heaven hath given thee a kingdom, power, and strength, and glory. And wheresoever the children of men dwell, the beasts of the field and the fowls of the heaven hath he given into thine hand, and hath made thee ruler over them all" (Dan. 2:37-38).

Again, he says to his son Belshazzar, "The most high God gave Nebuchadnezzar thy father a kingdom, and majesty, and glory, and honour: and for the majesty that he gave him, all people, nations, and languages, trembled and feared before him" (Dan. 5:18-19).

When we hear that the king was appointed by God, let us at the same time remember those divine commands concerning honoring and fearing the king, and we will have no doubt that we must view even the most iniquitous tyrant as occupying the place with which the Lord has honored him.

When Samuel declared to the people of Israel what they would suffer from their kings, he said, "This will be the manner of the king that shall reign over you: He will take your sons, and appoint them for himself, for his chariots, and to be his horsemen; and some shall run before his chariots. And he will appoint him captains over thousands, and captains over fifties; and will set them to ear his ground, and to reap his harvest, and to make his instruments of war, and instruments of his chariots. And he will take your daughters to be confectionaries, and to be cooks, and to be bakers. And he will take your fields, and your vineyards, and your oliveyards, even the best of them, and give them to his servants. And he will take the tenth of your seed, and of your vineyards, and give to his officers, and to his servants. And he will take your menservants, and your maidservants, and your goodliest young men, and your asses, and put them to his work. He will take the tenth of your sheep: and ye shall be his servants" (1 Sam. 8:11-17).

Certainly these things could not be done legally by kings, since the law held them bound to all restraint. But this was called justice in regard to the people because they were bound to obey and could not lawfully resist him. It's the same as if Samuel had said, "To such a degree kings will indulge in tyranny, but it is not for you to restrain them. The only thing remaining for you will be to receive their commands and be obedient to their words."

A LOOK AT NEBUCHADNEZZAR

But the most remarkable and well-known passage is in Jeremiah. Though it's rather long, I'm still going to quote it because it most clearly settles this whole question.

"I have made the earth, the man and the beast that are upon the ground, by my great power, and by my outstretched arm, and have given it unto whom it seemed meet unto me. And now have I given all these lands into the hand of Nebuchadnezzar the king of Babylon, my servant: and the beasts of the field have I given him also to serve him. And all nations shall serve him, and his son, and his son's son, until the very time of his land come: and then many nations and great kings shall serve themselves of him. And it shall come to pass, that the nation and kingdom which will not serve the same Nebuchadnezzer the king of Babylon, and that will not put their neck under the yoke of the king of Babylon, that nation will I punish, saith the Lord, with the sword, and with famine, and with pestilence, until I have consumed them by his hand" (Jer. 27:5-8). Therefore "bring your necks under the yoke of the king of Babylon, and serve him and his people, and live" (v. 12).

We see how great an obedience the Lord demanded to this dreadful and ferocious tyrant. And the only reason He did this is because this king held the position of authority in the kingdom. In other words, the divine decree had placed him on the throne of the kingdom and had elevated him to regal majesty, and this position could not be lawfully violated.

If we constantly keep before our eyes and minds the fact that even the most iniquitous kings are appointed by the same decree which establishes all regal authority, we will never entertain the seditious thought that a king is to be treated according to what he deserves. We will also remember that we are still bound to fulfill the role of good subjects even to him who on his part doesn't fulfill his role as a king to us.

GOD HAS APPOINTED ALL POSITIONS OF AUTHORITY

It is vain to object that this command was specifically given to the Israelites. For we must pay attention to the ground on which the Lord founds it: "I have given the kingdom to Nebuchadnezzar; therefore serve him and live." We mustn't doubt that we are bound to serve whoever has received the rule of the kingdom. Whenever God raises any one to royal honor, He declares that He has chosen this man to reign. We have clear declarations of this in Scripture.

Solomon says: "For the transgression of a land, many are the princes thereof" (Prov. 28:2). Job says: "He looseth the bond of kings, and girdeth their loins with a girdle" (Job 12:18). This being confessed, nothing remains for us but to serve him and live.

There is in Jeremiah another command in which the Lord thus orders His people: "Seek the peace of the city whither I have caused you to be carried away captives, and pray unto the Lord for it: for in the peace thereof shall ye have peace" (Jer. 29:7). Here the Israelites, plundered of all their property, torn from their homes, driven into exile, and thrown into miserable bondage, are ordered to pray for the prosperity of their conquerors—not as we are elsewhere ordered to pray for our persecutors, but that his kingdom might be preserved in safety and peace, that they also might live prosperously under him.

Thus David, when already king-elect by the ordination of God and anointed with His holy oil, though wrongly and unjustly assailed by Saul, holds the life of the king who sought his life to be sacred because the Lord had invested him with royal honor. "The Lord forbid that I should do this thing unto my master, the Lord's anointed, to stretch forth mine hand against him, seeing he is the anointed of the Lord." "Mine eyes spare thee; and I said, I will not put forth mine hand against my lord; for he is the Lord's anointed" (1 Sam. 24:6, 11).

Again: "Who can stretch forth his hand against the Lord's anointed, and be guiltless"? "As the Lord liveth, the Lord shall smite him; or his day shall come to die; or he shall descend into battle, and perish. The Lord forbid that I should stretch forth mine hand against the Lord's anointed" (1 Sam. 26:9-11).

CHAPTER ELEVEN

Duties of Subjects and Rulers

We owe all of our rulers a feeling of reverence, and even of piety, no matter what their characters may be. I repeat this so often in order that we might learn not to consider the individuals themselves but to consider it enough that the Lord has willed to impress and engrave His inviolable majesty upon such characters.

"But rulers," you will say, "owe mutual duties to those under them." I already stated this. But if you conclude from this that we are only obligated to obey righteous and just governors, you reason absurdly. Husbands are bound by mutual duties to their wives, and parents to their children. But if husbands and parents neglect their duty and if they are harsh and severe to the children whom they are commanded not to provoke to anger, and if by their severity they harass them beyond measure, are children any less bound to fulfill their duty to their parents? If husbands spitefully mistreat the wives they are commanded to love and to care for as the weaker vessels, should the wives cease to honor their husbands? They are still subject even to the wicked and negligent.

Indeed, our duty isn't to look behind us—that is, to inquire into the duties of one another—but to submit to our own duty. This ought especially to be exemplified in the case of those who are placed under the power of others. Therefore, if we are cruelly tormented by a savage ruler, if we are greedily pillaged by a covetous or rapacious man, if we are neglected by a lazy sluggard—if, in short, we are persecuted for righteousness' sake by an ungodly and profane ruler, let us first consider and remember our own sins, for doubtless the Lord is chastising us by such scourges. In this way, humility will put a restraint on our impatience.

And let us remember that it's not up to us to cure someone else's evils. All that remains for us is to implore the help of the Lord, for He holds in His hands the hearts of kings and the ways of nations. "God standeth in the congregation of the mighty; he judgeth among the gods." All kings and judges of the earth who have not kissed His anointed and who have enacted unjust laws to oppress the poor in judgment, and who work violence to the cause of the humble, who make widows a prey and plunder the fatherless, will fall and be crushed before His face.

GOD JUDGES TYRANTS BY MANY MEANS

In this, the goodness, power, and providence of God is wondrously displayed. Sometimes He raises up open avengers from among His own servants and gives them His command to punish accursed tyranny and deliver His people from calamity when they are unjustly oppressed. At other times He employs the fury of men for this purpose, even though they act with other thoughts and other aims than His. Thus, He rescued His people Israel from the tyranny of Pharaoh by Moses; from the violence of Chusa, king of Syria, by Othniel; and from other bondage by other kings or judges.

He also humbled the pride of Tyre by the Egyptians; the insolence of the Egyptians by the Assyrians; the ferocity of the Assyrians by the Chaldeans; the confidence of Babylon by the Medes and Persians—Cyrus having previously subdued the Medes; while the ingratitude of the kings of Judah and Israel and their wicked obstinacy after all His kindness, He subdued and punished at one time by the Assyrians, at another by the Babylonians.

All these things, however, were not done in the same way. The first group of deliverers were called by the lawful call of God to perform such deeds. When they took up arms against kings, they in no way transgressed that majesty with which kings are invested by divine appointment. Instead, being armed from heaven, they subdued a greater authority by means of a lesser authority, just like kings can lawfully punish their own subordinates.

The second group, though they were directed by the hand of God as seemed good to Him, and though they did His work without knowing it, yet they had nothing but evil in their thoughts and intentions.

LESSER MAGISTRATES ARE A DEFENSE OF FREEDOM

But whatever may be thought of the acts of the men themselves, the Lord executed His own work equally through them when He broke the bloody scepters of insolent kings and overthrew their unbearable tyrannies. Let rulers hear this and be afraid.

But, at the same time, let us guard ourselves most carefully against spurning or violating the honored and majestic authority of rulers, an authority which God has sanctioned by the surest edicts, even though those invested with it may be utterly unworthy of it and, as far as they are able, desecrate it by their iniquity. Although the Lord takes vengeance on unrestrained tyranny, yet we must not suppose that vengeance has been committed to us, to whom no command has been given except to obey and suffer.

I'm speaking only of private individuals here. For, when magistrates have been appointed by the people to restrain the tyranny of kings, I am in no way forbidding these to officially stop and restrain the undue license of kings.

WE MUST ALWAYS OBEY GOD ABOVE ALL

But, regarding the obedience that is due to the commands of rulers, we must always make one exception. Indeed, we must be particularly careful that these commands aren't incompatible with our obedience to Him. The wishes of all kings should be subject to His will, and all their commands must yield to Him.

Before His majesty, their scepters must bow.

And, indeed, how preposterous would it be to please men and thus incur the displeasure of Him for whose sake you obey men! The Lord, therefore, is King of kings. When He opens His sacred mouth, He alone is to be heard before all and above all.

We are subject to the men who rule over us, but we are subject to them only in the Lord. If they command anything against Him, we mustn't pay the least regard to it or be moved by all the dignity or authority which they possess as magistrates—a dignity to which no injury is done when it is subordinated to the special and truly supreme power of God. On this ground Daniel denies that he had sinned at all against the king when he refused to obey his wicked decree (Dan. 6:22). He said this because the king had exceeded his limits and had not only wronged men but, by raising himself against God, had virtually abrogated his own power.

On the other hand, the Israelites are condemned for having too quickly obeyed the wicked edict of their king. For, when Jeroboam made the golden calf, they forsook the temple of God and, in submission to their king, revolted to new idolatries (1 Kin. 12:28). Their descendents showed the same readiness to bow before the decrees of their kings. For this they are severely rebuked by the prophet (Hos. 5:11).

People hope to be praised for their modesty and submission when they declare that they must not disobey their kings, but this is merely a clever pretext to conceal their hypocrisy. The Lord has not abdicated His own rights to mortals by appointing them to rule over their fellowmen. Nor is His earthly power diminished when it is subjected to its Author, before whom even the principalities of heaven tremble as suppliants.

LET US NOT BE AFRAID OF WICKED RULERS

I know that subjects place themselves in imminent peril when they refuse to obey their rulers in this way, for kings are most indignant when they are disobeyed. As Solomon says, "The wrath of a king is as messengers of death" (Prov. 16:14). But, since Peter, one of heaven's heralds, has published the decree, "We ought to obey God rather than men" (Acts 5:29), let us console ourselves with the thought that we are rendering the obedience which the Lord requires. Let us endure anything rather than turn aside from godliness.

And, that our courage might not fail, Paul encourages us by the additional consideration that we were redeemed by Christ at the great price which our redemption cost Him, in order that we might not yield a slavish obedience to the depraved wishes of men, and far less be submissive to their wickedness (1 Cor. 7:23).

CHAPTER TWELVE

Magistrates Must Withstand and Resist All Evil

*So I turned and came down from the mount, and the
mount burned with fire: . . . And I looked, and, behold, ye
had sinned against the LORD your God, and had made you
a molten calf: ye had turned aside quickly out of the way
which the LORD had commanded you. . . . And the LORD
was very angry with Aaron to have destroyed him: and I
prayed for Aaron also the same time.*
Deuteronomy 9:15-20

After Moses had spoken of the sin that the people had
committed in making a golden calf to worship, he shows
that Aaron was to be blamed for that crime, even though
he had attempted to resist it. He didn't display such steadfastness
as he ought to have done as a ruler among the people. For
magistrates will have a much stricter account to make than those
who are private individuals. Therefore Aaron ought to have
taught the people and to have withstood their evil deeds even to
the death.

Now it's true that, when Aaron saw that the people were
determined to have an idol to worship, he told them it was wickedness to do so. And, when he realized that he couldn't stop
them, he tried another tack and labored to drive them from their
desire by demanding their jewels and ornaments and the things
which they considered most precious. For he thought that by this
means he could drive this foolishness out of their heads.

You see then that Aaron didn't consent to their evil but

did his best to stop it. However, he didn't do this with as much fortitude as he ought to have done. For he should instead have risked his life rather than consent to an idolatry by which God's honor and true worship was corrupted by transferring it to a puppet, a dead and senseless thing. Shouldn't Aaron have been zealous enough to have risked his own life rather than agree to this? Shouldn't he have laid down his life for Him, particularly since God had placed him in such an exalted position? For he was the high priest. And, even though he hadn't yet been consecrated to his office, yet he knew well enough what God had appointed him to. Therefore he had no excuse for what he did.

Now we must learn from this passage that those whom God has appointed to govern His people are not acquitted of their duty by merely refusing to consent to evil or by not being the authors of it. To the contrary, they must withstand it to the utmost and must possess such invincible steadfastness that they do not swerve aside from their duty, no matter how much people may beg them to do so. Even when they see terrible uprisings and rebellions, yet they must not allow their courage to fail. They must always stand firm for the right and good.

And, if they find themselves in danger, with no other recourse except to pray to God for His protection, yet they still must not turn aside from their duty to protect themselves. This is why Aaron would not have escaped unpunished—for God would certainly have punished him—if his brother Moses hadn't interceded for him.

We must not think nowadays that God has changed His mind. Instead, we must realize that all those who refuse to resist evil to the utmost will be caught up and included in the same condemnation as the evildoers, and God's vengeance will consume them all together. For, if a ruler allows evil to exist when he is able to prevent it, he subsidizes that evil. This is understood even by the heathen, who rebuke the negligence and indifference of their magistrates and officers of justice by their proverb: "If he who ought to restrain evil winks at it, it is exactly the same as if he sounded a trumpet to proclaim liberty and license to all evildoing—and he will be found guilty before God." Indeed, this proverb is so common as to teach us that God will not hold magistrates guiltless if they have been so negligent in fulfilling their duty and office.

Now, if the world condemns them, what will become of them when they appear before the Heavenly Judge? Thus, magistrates are here warned of their duty: when they see any evil, they must withstand it. Even if they don't possess sufficient worldly force, yet they must lay down their lives rather than yield to such wickedness and allow it to reign because of their cowardliness.

Let the lords of justice look well to themselves. For, even though men may acquit them, yet they won't be acquitted before God if they turn a blind eye and allow wickedness to prevail when they see God offended. If they see justice perverted and don't manfully withstand it, they will give an account for it. Besides this, God will also bring them to shame before the entire world so that they might experience beforehand the condemnation He has prepared for them. Therefore let every man diligently examine himself.

Let us also note in general that whoever refuses to withdraw themselves from the company of the wicked—even though they don't consent to their wickedness but merely refuse to withstand them in it—will be considered before God as accessories to the crime. We hear how Paul tells all believers, both great and small, "Have no fellowship with the unfruitful works of darkness, but rather reprove them" (Eph. 5:11). Thus, we must refrain from becoming partakers of evil, and we must openly declare that we will take no part in it.

But yet this still isn't enough, for we must also show ourselves to be enemies of the wicked and must stand against them. Those who refuse to do so are utter cowards, and their hypocrisy will be considered treason by God.

But what of all this? We see how the world works. For nowadays no friendship can be maintained unless people encourage their neighbors in their evildoing. Men mock God openly to His face, and yet you will find yourselves at open war with them if you refuse to approve and agree with them in every outrage against God. But, no matter what we see in the world, yet the Law will not be changed. We can harden ourselves in our wicked lifestyles as much as we like, but God will not fail to be our Judge—and He will certainly judge us according to this standard.

Therefore let us not think that He should change Himself when we give ourselves free license to engage in all kinds of evil and when we justify ourselves under the pretence that everyone else is doing it. We mustn't think that we will escape for all that. Instead, let us beware of being included and caught up in the same vengeance that God pronounces against sinners because we refuse to withstand them to the utmost of our power. Everyone— without exception—ought to do this (as I said before), yet those who are in authority must be very diligent in showing the way to all the others.

CHAPTER THIRTEEN

The Solemn Duty of Choosing Rulers

*Judges and officers shalt thou make thee in all thy gates,
which the LORD thy God giveth thee, throughout thy tribes:
and they shall judge the people with just judgment. Thou
shalt not wrest judgment; thou shalt not respect persons,
neither take a gift: for a gift doth blind the eyes of the wise,
and pervert the words of the righteous.*
Deuteronomy 16:18-19

If we had remained in the same integrity and perfection of nature in which God created us, the order of justice (or civil order, as men call it) wouldn't be so necessary for us, for every person would carry the law in his heart. Because of this, we wouldn't need to be compelled to do good, for we would each know the law and would with one accord follow what is good and just. Therefore law and justice is like a remedy against this corruption existing in mankind.

Whenever mention is made of earthly government and civil order, we must realize that in this we have a mirror of our own perversity, for we are so wicked that force must be used to make us follow justice and reason. For why do those in authority bear a sword in their hand? They do this to quell and suppress those who rise up in wickedness and lawlessness (Rom. 13:4; 1 Pet. 2:14). And what is the reason for this? Simply that, though people ought of themselves to seek what is good and just, yet instead they pervert it and attempt to throw the whole world into confusion if they aren't stopped.

This is indeed most shameful, for God created us in His own image and gave us dominion and rule over all His creatures, and yet we must be driven by force because of our wickedness (Gen. 1:28). If you could pick out the most despised man in the world, yet he still carries in himself the image of God and this mark of dominion. Yet, even so, we are forced to be subjects because of our wickedness, as I just mentioned.

Thus, we must understand that God has not established the order of earthly government without good reason, for He recognized the corruption within us. This provides a clear warning to us to humble ourselves, considering that our sins require such a remedy. But yet we should also magnify God's goodness, for He chose to provide for us in such a way that all would not be utter confusion and chaos and that we might not turn the world upside down and ruin everything—as would certainly happen if we were left to ourselves.

For, if the strongest won the day, what would happen? It would be much better for us to live in the jungles with the wolves and savage beasts rather than dwell together among men if we were left to rule ourselves, for there is no beast on earth as fierce as our inordinate lusts and desires.

Therefore we must acknowledge the wonderful goodness of our God, who had such concern for us and our preservation that, since we couldn't maintain life unless we had laws to restrain us and judges to execute what was written in these laws, He provided for everything. By this we are also taught to love the civil order, knowing that it is a special gift of God and is a means of preserving mankind.

If we love the light of the sun because we can't live without it, and if we love bread and whatever else provides sustenance for us, let us also love the order of justice. For it would do us no good to have food and drink and all other things if we didn't also have laws and magistrates, for without them we would be stripped of all God's other blessings. Indeed, it would be better for us to have died on the day of our birth rather than to devour each other because of a lack of justice.

Thus we must consider this civil order as a testimony of God's grace, and we must treat it with as much honor as is due it. And let us each—as much as we are able—seek to uphold it, for we reveal ourselves to be deadly enemies of peace and the common good if we refuse to love justice and the civil order. And all those who trouble it and who attempt to pervert it are the worst of villains and ought to be considered enemies of the wellbeing of mankind. So wicked are they that we should all fight against them when we see them attempt to overturn justice and bring in such horrible confusion among us.

THE BLESSING OF CHOOSING ONE'S MAGISTRATES

Now there is good reason why it's here repeated that the people should establish judges and magistrates throughout the land after they entered it, even though we already expounded this in the first chapter (Deut. 1:13-14). God had good reason to repeat it here again, for He intends to show us that it does no good to have good and just laws unless we also have men appointed to enforce them and put them into execution. This was mentioned previously, but we must refresh our memories again. For we see that God speaks about the same thing many times so that we might make a greater consideration of it and spend more time meditating on it, and not forget it.

Even so, He now confirms the former words He spoke concerning magistrates. And, indeed, the common proverb has good reason to call them the soul or life of the law. For what good are all the laws and statutes in the world? They're nothing more than dead letters. They're recorded on paper, but they're not worth a thing unless we have men elected to put them into execution and to see that they are obeyed.

Thus you see what God means here by saying: "Judges and officers shalt thou make thee" (Deut. 16:18). He wanted them to choose the men. Surely such freedom was a singular gift. In fact, we see that it isn't granted to all people. Where princes rule, they appoint judges according to their own pleasure and liking, and ambition bears sway there—so much so that a courtier in the king's favor not only obtains offices for himself but also distributes them to others at his own appointment. But the corruption can be even greater and more shameful than this, for offices today are put up for sale just like any other kind of merchandise.

Therefore, since we have such examples, we must consider it an inestimable gift when God grants a people or nation the liberty to choose their own judges and magistrates. Indeed, when God gave that privilege to the Jews, it was a ratification of His adoption of them and His choosing them to be His heritage. For He intended them to be in a better and more excellent state than any of their neighbors who had kings and princes and no such freedom at all as they enjoyed.

Now, since this ought to be held in such great esteem, so also those who enjoy such a blessing must use it with a good and pure conscience. For why does our Lord deprive us of His blessings? Doesn't He do it because we have corrupted His gift by our abuse of it? We know quite well that whatever God gives us is desirable, for we see the benefit of it. Yet, instead of using it in a holy way, with thanksgiving, we instead make it serve our lusts. Now, when God sees His blessings turned to such wicked uses, and when He sees us employ them for the opposite reason He gave them, He takes them away from us.

Have we been deprived of them? We see this happen, and we think it strange; yet we don't consider how long God has borne with us. And we don't realize that He won't allow His gifts to be abused and mocked forever. Let us learn, therefore, that whenever God gives us any blessing, we must maintain it by our good and pure use of it. For in this way the possession will become permanent, if we don't pollute what God has given us for our profit.

Therefore, if we have the liberty to elect judges and magistrates, as much as it is an excellent gift (as I said before), let us preserve this liberty and employ it with a clean conscience. When a people possesses this privilege, let them be careful when they establish judges, for these men will be like lieutenants of God. Therefore no man should be chosen who can be bribed or who is already known to be a wicked man or incapable of upholding such a charge. But you must consider and discern those who are suited for this office, as if they were marked out by God.

And, because we don't have sufficient discernment to know whom to elect, we must turn to God in prayer. For it isn't enough for us to simply seek out those who are suitable and sufficient to execute their office. But, because we might be deceived—either because of our own weakness or because of the hypocrisy of men—and, after we make our best inquiry and search, we choose the wrong man, therefore let us ask God to overrule all and to give us His wisdom and discretion. This is what we must learn from this verse about choosing and appointing judges and magistrates.

CHAPTER FOURTEEN

Qualifications of a True Magistrate

*Judges and officers shalt thou make thee in all thy gates,
which the LORD thy God giveth thee, throughout thy tribes:
and they shall judge the people with just judgment. Thou
shalt not wrest judgment; thou shalt not respect persons,
neither take a gift: for a gift doth blind the eyes of the wise,
and pervert the words of the righteous.*
Deuteronomy 16:18-19

Now, it's expressly stated: "in all thy gates" or cities (Deut. 16:18). For what would happen if people were required to travel far away to seek justice when injustice is committed everywhere? Since crimes are frequent and touch us personally, if we had to go far to seek redress, we would scarcely benefit from this at all. A hundred crimes would be committed before we were able to bring the first one to justice. This is why our Lord said that judges and magistrates should be chosen in every city or village. It's as if He said that men always stand in need of some check.

I already said that we were created in the image of God and ought to rule over all creatures, but yet instead we need to be held in subjection ourselves. For, since we've perverted the order of nature, God must also cut us short to show how incapable we are of exercising dominion. Indeed, we're so unable to bear liberty that He must place us in subjection. Thus, let us learn that wherever corruption and vice exist, we must redress it immediately and in the same place.

It's true that there was a supreme court of justice in Judah. We also saw in the fifth chapter that difficult cases and matters of great importance were referred to Moses himself (Ex. 18:26). Yet God desired there to be order everywhere, so that if any disorder were committed, it could be dealt with immediately without requiring the parties to journey any great distance to seek justice. Indeed, judges and magistrates ought to watch out for crimes. They shouldn't sit back and wait until someone calls or demands their services, but they should punish evil whenever they see it.

I say *whenever they see it* because they ought to keep watch and pay attention. It isn't enough for a magistrate to punish what he knows to be wicked; he must also make diligent inquiry into these matters, as we've seen in other places (Deut. 13:14). If this were done, matters would be in much better order. This is what we must learn from our Lord desiring to have judges and magistrates in every city. If this weren't the case, many evils would be committed before a correction could be put in place, and thus the remedy would come too late, as we already mentioned.

Moving on, when Moses adds: "they shall judge the people with just judgment," he does this to confirm what he just said, which is (first of all) that men can't govern themselves but must have authorities to guide them, which is plainly expressed concerning the Jews, whom God had chosen over all other nations. Thus, let us understand that we have good reason to be deprived of the liberty that God established in mankind. Why is this? It's because we transform good into evil. Thus He must take it away from us.

A healthy man is at liberty to eat whatever he wants, and he won't show much concern about what he eats. He doesn't need a doctor to tell him not to eat such and such a food or to tell him not to drink this particular drink. But if a person is sick, he must follow his doctor's orders and must refrain from eating certain things. He must be held in check just like a little child and refrain from eating according to his desires. If a master is sick and commands his servant to bring him a particular thing he isn't allowed to eat, the servant will reply, "I dare not do it."

Thus we see that the sick are in subjection even to their own servants and can't do whatever they like. Why is this? It's because they aren't able to judge properly for themselves; their illness has taken control of them. Therefore they must be submissive.

So it is also with us. If we were healthy and perfect, God would use some other method to lead us. But, because we are so corrupt, He must restrain us and repress us in this way, as we already said. Thus we have the first point.

Secondly, Moses declares and stipulates what I said about election, that we must not place in the seat God has dedicated to Himself men who will overturn everything. For, if we elected to public office men who lead a wicked life, who have no fear of God or any honesty or uprightness, but are instead dissolute, lewd, and disorderly, who have no more wisdom than donkeys—in short, who are utterly insane—if we put such men in public office, we aren't dishonoring men but are engaging in high treason against God, for this is a defilement of His throne. Thus, we would do well to heed what Moses says here.

When it comes to electing magistrates, we mustn't make idols of men, and we mustn't judge them flippantly. Why? Because we dishonor God when we set in His place men who are unworthy of even having the rule of a single house. When we see a man who isn't even able to govern his own house, we don't put any trust in such a person. "What a fool!" someone will say of him. "He's utterly devoid of reason. He must be out of his mind, for he doesn't even know how to rule his own house and family." And will we place such a man in the seat of justice?

Here's a man who can't live peaceably with his wife—and do we think he'll be able to maintain the peace in an entire city? Or someone will recommend that he be elected to the city council. To what purpose? To uphold peace. And how can that be? Right now he only has a wife and household to govern, and he can't even do that! When he's at home, he can't even lead his wife and children.

Thus, when such things happen, God is openly despised. Therefore we ought to pay even more diligent heed to what

Moses says here: electing judges and magistrates isn't a mere formality or ceremony but is a sacred task in which we ought to engage with all reverence. God hasn't placed such a yoke on any people's neck to say, "Choose whoever you want. Make as flippant a choice as you desire." No, but He instead lists the qualifications of these men and points them out with His finger. "Beware," He says, "and exercise discretion and wisdom when choosing men to govern the people." For this word "judge" means the same as "to govern."

Secondly, He says, "they shall judge the people *with just judgment.*" When He speaks of judging or governing, He does so intentionally and with good reason. For there is no point in choosing those who need to be taught. If these men need to be tutored in their job, should we elect them to govern others? This would be a most grievous mockery to God. Again, this is a matter of justice and uprightness. To choose men before they are tried and well proved would be a definite corruption of all good order.

This is where so many tumults and revolutions come from. We're shocked to see our Lord overthrow nations, and we watch in astonishment as nations that once enjoyed liberty are overwhelmed and oppressed by tyranny, but we don't consider what started all these things. The root of it was the abuse committed because the people didn't seek to preserve the state God had established among them. Nor did each of them faithfully fulfill the duty commanded them. Thus, let us be even more diligent to remember what is taught us here.

CHAPTER FIFTEEN

Perverting Justice by Fearing Men

After having said that, Moses adds "Thou shalt not wrest judgment; thou shalt not respect persons, neither take a gift." Then he adds the reason for this: "for a gift doth blind the eyes of the wise, and pervert the words of the righteous" (Deut. 16:19).

He sets down in the first place the general rule: we must not wrest or pervert justice. We can indeed compare justice to a straight line. If it bends to one side or the other, this is iniquity. Therefore Moses says, "Don't turn justice aside." That is, "Keep your eye on the line of justice. Follow it perfectly, without swerving to either one side or the other."

Then he shows how this is done: we must not favor particular people, and we must not be given to corruption. For, when we consider a deed simply in itself, even nature teaches us what should be done. It's true that we still always need to call on God, for we see what weakness exists in our minds. For we are often stone blind even in the clearest and most evident matters. Thus, we must not trust in our own minds or consider ourselves wise enough to judge what is set before us by our own wisdom. We must recognize that this is a heavenly gift, just as Solomon declares (Eccl. 2:26).

And, if we are deceived in even the smallest matters, what will happen when it's a question of pronouncing judgment on the most important issues? Thus, judges much first humble themselves and recognize that, if they aren't governed by the Spirit of God, they will never know how to judge rightly.

Therefore they must submit themselves to Him and must ask counsel from Him, that they might be taught by His Word and might give themselves to His Spirit, to whom they must submit themselves.

THE DANGER OF REGARDING PERSONS IN JUDGMENT

Next, Moses desires to show the main reasons for all the corruptions existing in justice. For, as I already mentioned, if we look only to the deed, without considering the persons and without being concerned about favor or hatred, we will know how to give a just sentence. If we could always judge like this, the litigants would never need to appear in court, and we'd never need to know who the plaintiff and the defendant were, so that the judges wouldn't be tempted or carried away by bribery, flattery, lies, or other similar things; but the case could be laid before them simply and nakedly as it is. Then we would never see what we all see daily right now, which is that people can generally never obtain right or justice.

For, by nature (as I said) we are taught to say, "This is good, this is just, this is upright." But, as soon as the parties appear before us and we see that some of them are our neighbors or friends; or that one of them is a great man or a rich man and the other a poor man; and when one side seeks to win their case by threats and the other by sweet words and presents—and bribery comes trotting in behind—suddenly everything is turned upside down, and those who could see clearly beforehand now can't see at all and find themselves utterly blind.

Therefore let us note that it should have been quite enough to have merely said in a single statement that we must not pervert justice. But we are so prone to evil that we will naturally fall into it if we aren't explicitly told how and by what means we must maintain ourselves in integrity and uprightness—that is, by not considering individual people and by avoiding all desires to receive gifts and bribes.

Now, concerning the people, I've expounded this in other

places already (Deut. 1:17). We must not respect or consider whether a person is rich or poor, important or common, a stranger or a citizen, and similar things. For the word *person* means the same in Hebrew as how we would use it in our own language when we say, "Here's a person," that is, "Here's a man" or "Here's a member of mankind."

The word that Moses uses here in Hebrew can also mean a *face* or *countenance*. Thus, we mustn't consider the face of the person. What does that mean? It means the things that are visible and seen, the state, appearance, or outward look of a person. This word *appearance* also expresses Moses' meaning quite well. For, if I see a man poor, I may despise him. If I see a rich man, I show him honor. If I see a man of authority, I stand in fear of him. If I see a wretched lout, I pay no attention to him and scorn the sight of him. You see how the outward appearance spoils everything.

If I see a man who is able to please me—oh! I'll agree with him so that he can repay me for it. If I see another who can do me neither good nor harm—oh, I don't care what happens to him. Then, if I see someone whom I can injure to my own advantage, I'll do it. Why? Because my mind looks no further than the outward appearance. Now we see Moses' meaning. I've already spoken of all this in the first chapter of this book, but the Holy Spirit had very good reason to repeat it here again.

In summary, let us learn that those who look at the outward appearance and who have no regard except to the person won't know how to walk in an upright and just way. Either they will be moved by fear or by favor and will give the victory to the wicked person who stands in the wrong. Why is this? Because they stand in fear that he will avenge himself if they condemn him. On the other hand, they hope for rewards if they favor him.

Therefore let us first of all remember that God requires steadfastness and courage in those who serve as judges. If they see a rich man who is considered to be a man of honor, let them take him for what he is—but yet they must still judge the case as it requires. But this steadfastness of mind is scarcely ever to be found. For, even though judges determine within themselves to follow the law, yet, because of all the blows they receive, they are often seized with such timidity that they become demoralized when they most need to stand for what is right. This is another reason why those who sit in the seat of justice must appeal to God and must diligently ask Him to strengthen them so that they might not be like reeds, shaken with every wind, but might openly follow the course God has appointed them, without bending or bowing in any way at all.

Let us then note first that we must possess such steadfastness that we aren't afraid at the sight of anyone's power or outward appearance. We must not let anyone's authority or riches alter our opinion of them, but we must remain firm so that the case always stands secure, without allowing such things to dazzle our eyes or say: "This is an important man; therefore I must favor him."

On the other hand, I also said that we must not despite a person who is contemptible in men's eyes. "Here's a man of little worth. It seems to me that I could render him an injustice without worrying about it." We often find ourselves in this position. If we're dealing with a man of no reputation, we think ourselves at liberty to say: "I know I did him wrong, but he's nobody of importance, so it really doesn't matter, and nobody's going to complain about it." But God desires justice and equity to be administered to all persons.

Therefore let those who find themselves in positions of honor consider that, if they despise the little people and those who appear to be rejected by everyone, they will still have to give an account of this. For, if God condescends to consider such people, and if He cares for them, and—even more!—if He calls Himself their protector, will He allow anyone to trample them underfoot and oppress and tyrannize them without avenging them? (Ps. 116:6.) So then, judges must be both steadfast and humane and must condescend to the lowliest people. They must receive such into their protection and must look out for and sustain them when they have a good and just cause. This is what we must learn from this verse.

Now, if this law were properly obeyed, we wouldn't have nearly as many complaints or lawsuits. Nor would things be in such confusion. But what do we have? We see a good judgment given and a fault or offense punished as it ought to be. Then we turn, and suddenly we see the same case go unpunished. Why is this? It's because the judges are considering the appearance of the persons. Here's a case where a judge is convinced of what verdict he must render. It's all very clear, he sees it, and he must award some punishment. This is done. But why isn't the same thing done in all other similar cases? Oh, that's because this side is favored over that one.

Indeed, men seek many pretenses and justifications for what they do, but this only makes the matter worse. God will not be deceived, no matter what subterfuge you employ. Yet we all see how this regard for persons perverts all true justice, and how prevalent this is on all sides. It's so common that a man is often acquitted in a case that is quite clear and patent in itself—if you don't consider the position of the people involved. But the judges, hindered by their consideration for the people involved, throw themselves into all kinds of doubts where no doubt ought to exist at all. Why is this? It's all due to this respect for persons.

Thus, we can see how great the wickedness of men is in this regard. But, no matter how wicked men are, our Lord doesn't want us to miss the instruction He gave to His people here. We mustn't allow it to become lost or unprofitable. Therefore let us be diligent to benefit from it.

We must also note that, just as judges and magistrates are forbidden to have any respect of persons, this exhortation applies to all of us. For why do we so often fail in our duties? Isn't it because we fall prey to this same respecting of persons? Therefore we must possess such steadfast courage that no greatness, pomp, authority, or worldly honors will win us over and pervert us. And, on the other hand, we must have meekness enough not to despise the lowliest of men, but must instead be righteous in our reception of them. That's what we should learn from this word *person*.

CHAPTER SIXTEEN

Blinding the Eyes of Justice

Thou shalt not wrest judgment; thou shalt not respect
persons, neither take a gift: for a gift doth blind the eyes of
the wise, and pervert the words of the righteous.
Deuteronomy 16:19

Now we have a second point. This one concerns gifts and bribery. "Thou shalt not take them," says the Lord. He doesn't say, "Thou shalt not sell justice," but He says, "Thou shalt not take them." Why is this? He adds the reason: "for a gift doth blind the eyes of the wise, and pervert the words of the righteous." Here is a reason well worth noting. It seems at first sight that for a judge to receive some gift wouldn't necessarily be evil or something to be condemned. But He's speaking here of presents or gifts that are given in respect to some case waiting to be heard.

For example, a criminal is attempting to escape punishment, so he tries to win the judge over to his side by sending him a present. Or another man puts himself forward and, in an attempt to obtain victory over his opponent, offers the judge a gift. Now our Lord didn't say, "When you receive a gift, beware of favoring the side that gave it to you. This would be wrong and would be putting justice up for sale." God doesn't speak in this way. Instead, He says, "Beware of taking it," for it's impossible for anyone who receives a gift to remain fully upright and not bend toward one side or the other.

MAKING GOD A LIAR

Now it's true that there are many who will say, "Oh, I don't need to worry about that. For myself, even though I accept the gift, yet I don't turn aside from fulfilling my duty. For, after I've received gifts from both sides, I'll pronounce judgment against the person who thought to bribe me by his gifts. There's no evil in that, is there? He was a fool to bring it to me, wasn't he? If he brings something, I'll accept it. But I certainly won't turn aside from my duty."

Such people attempt to make God a liar. We see here that He says that gifts blind the eyes of the wise. If a person thinks himself so sharp-sighted that he can receive gifts without clouding his vision, God says the complete opposite. If that person thinks he's so strong that he won't bend or turn aside, God declares that his resolve will be utterly destroyed when he receives a gift, so much so that no integrity will remain within him.

Thus it's a mockery to say, "I'll take it, but I'll still be careful not to turn aside or bend." This is utterly impossible, for it would make God a liar in this passage. Thus we see what we must first remember concerning this point.

Let those who are in the seat of justice consider this: "This man just brought me a present. Did he do it out of goodwill, as one neighbor to another or as a friend gives to his friend? Or is he bringing this because of some case that is going to come before me?"

For, if a man has a case brought before a judge and that judge receives something from him, he has offended God. Why? Because God has forbidden him to do this—and God knows why He issued this command. It isn't man's place to say, "It really doesn't matter; I'll be careful not to be corrupted by it." If we act in this way, we are tempting God, and He will mock at our presumption and will reveal that we are not such steadfast men as we think ourselves to be. He will show us that He had very good reason to say exactly what He said: when we have fingers stretched out and aching to receive a gift, and when we receive it, we blind ourselves and entangle our hearts in such a way that wisdom and uprightness are no longer found within us.

When God says something, we must not reply to the contrary. Indeed, those who boast of being so steadfast that they could never be corrupted or induced to bend by receiving gifts don't need to be brought before God to be convinced of their error. Even the smallest children can judge such a case. This is such a common thing that I could give you very well-known examples of it.

Thus, since our Lord warns us that we will be blinded if we receive bribes, let us beware of this. Unless we desire to willingly poison ourselves, we must observe this law. Judges must never receive anything, at least not from anyone who is appearing in judgment before them. They must refrain from this unless they desire to turn aside from all lawful order and justice.

GOD'S MERCY IN SUPPLYING OUR NEEDS
AND CLEANSING OUR INIQUITIES

By this we see how our Lord, who knows our diseases, immediately applies suitable and fitting remedies to them. What then remains for us to do? We must each make a close examination of ourselves and must search ourselves carefully. The reason why we are so presumptuous as to tempt God is because we don't enter into ourselves and consider how wicked we are. Nor do we consider our many weaknesses. But, if we did carefully consider ourselves, we would each realize: "Alas! It wouldn't take anything to pervert me, for I am the weakest thing in the world! Even if I have no outside temptation to sway me, yet there's enough wickedness in myself to do it. What will happen when an evil opportunity arises? I'll stumble and fall."

Thus, if we are aware of our own wickedness, we'll certainly seek as much assistance as we can possibly obtain to preserve us. Now, since God has provided this and has shows us on one hand how weak and frail we are, and on the other hand how we can fall into such wickedness and sin, He says, "My friends, it's true that you are subject to evil. But here is how you will be preserved: Refrain from such a thing. Accept the remedy I give you."

I ask you, when our Lord speaks so tenderly to us, if we refuse this, won't our ingratitude deserve to be punished by delivering us up to all evil and allowing Satan to drive us and carry us away? Wouldn't we deserve to have God forsake us and allow us to fall into such grave sins that the entire world would hold us in horror?

Therefore we ought to be most diligent in noting this passage, for God isn't here speaking of the wicked and foolish but of the wise and righteous. This is such a terrifying thing that it ought to make our hair stand on end. Why? Because gifts and bribes are so corrupting that they blind the eyes of those who possess wisdom and discretion. Now, these things are certainly an inestimable gift of God.

When we speak of wisdom, we mustn't think that it grows out of men's brains. No, it is God who gives it (Jas. 1:5). It is God who gives certain men good minds and leads them in such a way that they walk in righteous and praiseworthy ways. Yet, if God were to let such people alone, and if they once accepted this corruption of gifts, not only would the wisdom that God has given them be obscured, but it would also be utterly blinded.

Therefore, as Paul says, let us beware, and let us look to ourselves lest we also fall (1 Cor. 10:12). For our Lord employs a hideous threat here when He says that those who see clearly will become blind if they allow themselves to receive gifts. Those who are upright and holy will be perverted and will turn to all evil. When we hear this, shouldn't we be on our guard and keep a good watch over ourselves lest we be surprised by Satan's wiles? Let us therefore prepare for these temptations long before they come upon us. And, when we see our Lord warning us in this way, let us fear, and let us not rush against Him willfully or give way to stubbornness. Let us instead consider that even those who appear to be as righteous as the angels would be overthrown and fall if they give themselves to this.

Therefore let us learn to restrain ourselves and keep ourselves on a short rein and submit ourselves to the Lord's rule. Then we needn't fear, for if He wills to give us wisdom and discretion, He will increase it more and more in us and will keep us in it until the end, as long as we always seek it from Him and pray continually for Him to preserve it within us, as I said before.

CHAPTER SEVENTEEN

A Time for Repentance

*Moreover all these curses shall come upon thee, and shall
pursue thee, and overtake thee, till thou be destroyed;
because thou hearkenedst not unto the voice of the LORD
thy God, to keep his commandments and his statutes which
he commanded thee: and they shall be upon thee for a sign
and for a wonder, and upon thy seed for ever. Because thou
servedst not the LORD thy God with joyfulness, and with
gladness of heart, for the abundance of all things; therefore
shalt thou serve thine enemies which the LORD shall send
against thee, in hunger, and in thirst, and in nakedness, and
in want of all things: and he shall put a yoke of iron upon
thy neck, until he have destroyed thee. The LORD shall bring
a nation against thee from far, from the end of the earth, as
swift as the eagle flieth; a nation whose tongue thou shalt not
understand; a nation of fierce countenance, which shall not
regard the person of the old, nor shew favour to the young.*
Deuteronomy 28:45-50

Let us diligently note what is said here, which is that God
will raise up a foreign people against those who refuse
to be subject to Him. God rules over us in such a way
that He desires to be a Father to us rather than a king or ruler
bringing vengeance. It's true that we must pay homage to Him
as to our sovereign King and that we must live as His people in
all submission and humility, ordering our lives in obedience to
Him. But yet He still performs the office of a father to us and
chooses to be known as our Father. For He speaks in a kind way.

Even though His commandments are difficult because of the wickedness and rebellion within our sinful flesh, yet after our Lord reveals His will to us, He exhorts, warns, and admonishes us, and He always does so with such gentle kindness that we would have to be devoid of all sense and reason if we didn't turn such goodness to our own profit.

Now, will we listen to our God when He speaks to us in such a sweet and gracious way? If we don't, He will speak to us through harsh blows of swords, spears, and firearms. We won't understand this, for the language is very foreign to our ears. Why does He do this? We didn't listen when God spoke graciously to us—indeed, even when He stooped down to teach us like little children are taught their ABCs.

Thus, let us realize that when we turn a deaf ear to God, He will speak to us in another language and will stir up foreigners and insolent, shameless people who will show no reverence and no justice or fair dealing. And, when you beg them to have pity and compassion on you, they won't pay any attention to your pleas. You will then find yourselves in more dire straits than you have ever experienced.

And what is the remedy for all these calamities? We must enter—indeed, we must enter into our own consciences and not gnash our teeth against men (as we are accustomed to do), nor set ourselves against them. For our battle isn't located there. Instead, we must realize that God has chosen to chastise us through these men because we have been so hardheaded and have refused to be instructed by His Word, which was His reason for giving it.

Thus, let us profit from all these adversities and corrections that God sends upon us. Indeed, let's not wait until we feel His blows. But, when God gives us the grace of instructing us at the expense of someone else, let us profit from this. And, if He spares us, let us not abuse His patience.

And, since the means of reconciling ourselves to Him is by embracing the promise He offers us in the Gospel, let us embrace our Lord Jesus Christ, who is our peace, in order that we might be dealt with in a fatherly way at the hands of God (Eph. 2:14).

Now let us bow before the majesty of our good God, acknowledging our sins and asking Him to make us feel them more and more, but also that He might bear with us in such a way that His chastisements and corrections might be fatherly and that He might not punish us beyond measure. May this drive us to the obedience of His justice and righteousness, and may He always supply us such consolation that we can ever rejoice in Him and glorify Him for procuring our salvation through such varied means.

A Light to My Path:
An Exposition of the Ten Commandments

by John Calvin
translated by R. A. Sheats

Softcover, 204 pages

A Light to My Path is a new translation of a collection of twelve sermons that Reformer John Calvin preached on the Ten Commandments.

Warm and earnest in tone, showing profound scholarship yet with an emphasis on practical application, Calvin's sermons on the Ten Commandments unite a theological depth with a down-to-earth, easily-understandable style, offering the modern reader an easy and enjoyable access to the riches of Calvin's theology and understanding of the Scriptures.

The Christian and the Magistrate:
Roles, Responsibilities, and Jurisdictions

by Pierre Viret
translated by R. A. Sheats

Softcover, 132 pages

What's the biblical definition of a civil magistrate? Should Christians be subject to them? Should civil governments be subject to God? Is physical resistance to authority ever lawful? Under what circumstances? And what is a Christian's role with respect the civil realm?

16th century Swiss Reformer Pierre Viret addresses these and other issues in this superb collection of writings on the applications of biblical truths pertaining to civil magistrates and the Christian's duty to them.

PIERRE VIRET:
The Angel of the Reformation

by R. A. Sheats

Hardcover, illustrated, 323 pages
ISBN: 978-098437817

For the first time in five hundred years, a full biography of Pierre Viret is now available to the English-speaking world. Packed with fascinating details and bristling with original documents and letters of the Reformers, the history of this forgotten giant of the Reformation is recounted in an interesting and enthralling way. Known by his contemporaries as *the Angel of the Reformation*, Viret was truly a radiant 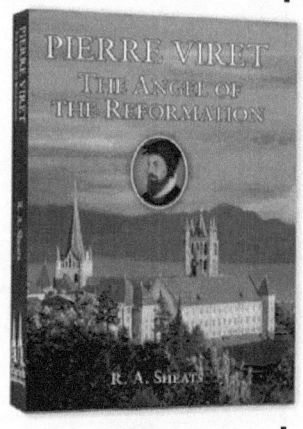 light amongst the men of his generation, a light which has finally been uncovered in this our day. May the unveiling of this precious life inspire and equip a new generation of Reformers as they seek to extend God's glory to every area of human existence!

"R. A. Sheats has written a superb biography on our Swiss Reformer that is both warmhearted and scholarly. We anticipate a soon translation into French."

- **Daniel Bovet**, President of *l'Association Pierre Viret*, Switzerland

Letters of Comfort
to the Persecuted Church

by Pierre Viret
translated by R. A. Sheats

Softcover, 114 pages

From the depths of a pastor's heart
come letters of hearty biblical comfort for persecuted believers. Written to men and women facing im-
prisonment, banishment, suffering,
and death, these letters capture the
heart of the Gospel and offer consolation and sincere comfort for those
suffering for the sake of Christ.

Written by Pierre Viret (1511-1571),
a Swiss Reformer and close friend of
John Calvin, these letters overflow
with a pastoral concern for the souls as well as the physical
needs of his readers. Republished several times throughout
the Reformation era, Viret's letters appear now for the first
time in the English language, and the comfort they offer to
an afflicted church is as pertinent today as it was the day he
wrote them.